Research Reports on College Transitions | No. 5

An Exploration of Intersecting Identities of First-Generation, Low-Income Students

Rashné R. Jehangir, Michael J. Stebleton, and Veronica Deenanath

Cite as:

Jehangir, R. R., Stebleton, M. J., & Deenanath, V. (2015). *An exploration of intersecting identities of first-generation, low-income college students* (Research Report No. 5). Columbia, SC: University of South Carolina, National Resource Center for The First-Year Experience and Students in Transition.

ISBN: 978-1-889271-97-2
Published by:
National Resource Center for The First-Year Experience® and Students in Transition
University of South Carolina
1728 College Street, Columbia, SC 29208
www.sc.edu/fye

Production Staff for the National Resource Center:

Project Manager:	Toni Vakos, Editor
Design and Production:	Allison Minsk, Graphic Artist
External Reviewer:	Ani Yazedjian, Chair and Professor, Family and Consumer Sciences, Illinois State University

---

Library of Congress Cataloging-in-Publication Data

Jehangir, Rashné Rustom, 1970-
  An exploration of intersecting identities of first-generation, low-income college students / Rashné R. Jehangir, Michael J. Stebleton, Veronica Deenanath.
  pages cm -- (Research report on college transition ; no. 5)
  Includes bibliographical references.
  ISBN 978-1-889271-97-2
  1. First-generation college students--Minnesota--Minneapolis--Case studies. 2. People with social disabilities--Education (Higher)--Minnesota--Minneapolis--Case studies. 3. University of Minnesota--Students--Case studies. I. Title.
  LC4069.6.J45 2015
  378.1'98209776'579--dc23
                    2015017552

About the Publisher

The National Resource Center for The First-Year Experience and Students in Transition was born out of the success of University of South Carolina's much-honored University 101 course and a series of annual conferences on the freshman-year experience. The momentum created by the educators attending these early conferences paved the way for the development of the National Resource Center, which was established at the University of South Carolina in 1986. As the National Resource Center broadened its focus to include other significant student transitions in higher education, it underwent several name changes, adopting the National Resource Center for The First-Year Experience and Students in Transition in 1998.

Today, the Center collaborates with its institutional partner, University 101 Programs, in pursuit of its mission to advance and support efforts to improve student learning and transitions into and through higher education. We achieve this mission by providing opportunities for the exchange of practical and scholarly information as well as the discussion of trends and issues in our field through convening conferences and other professional development events, such as institutes, workshops, and online learning opportunities; publishing scholarly practice books, research reports, a peer-reviewed journal, electronic newsletters, and guides; generating, supporting, and disseminating research and scholarship; hosting visiting scholars; and maintaining several online channels for resource sharing and communication, including a dynamic website, listservs, and social media outlets. The National Resource Center serves as the trusted expert, internationally recognized leader, and clearinghouse for scholarship, policy, and best practice for all postsecondary student transitions.

Institutional Home

The National Resource Center is located at the University of South Carolina's (UofSC) flagship campus in Columbia. Chartered in 1801, the University's mission is twofold: (a) to establish and maintain excellence in its student population, faculty, academic programs, living and learning environment, technological infrastructure, library resources, research and scholarship, public and private support, and endowment; and (b) to enhance the industrial, economic, and cultural potential of the state. The Columbia campus offers 324 degree programs through its 14 degree-granting colleges and schools. Students have been awarded more than $20 million for national scholarships and fellowships since 1994. In fiscal year 2014, faculty generated $230 million in funding for research, outreach, and training programs. UofSC is one of only 63 public universities listed by the Carnegie Foundation in the highest tier of research institutions in the United States.

Acknowledgements

The authors of this manuscript would like to thank our colleague Steven Cisneros for his critical role in co-facilitating the focus groups for this study. In addition, we acknowledge the hard work of McNair Scholar Aliya Jeylani who spent the summer of 2011 immersed in this project—scheduling the focus groups, transcribing the digital recordings, and assisting in preliminary analysis of the data.

Contents

Introduction

During the past 20 years, and especially the last five, there has been significant growth in the number of first-generation (FG) students who have entered the academy (Peabody, Hutchens, Lewis, & Deffendall, 2011). In 2007, approximately 17% of entering first-year students were first-generation, but today, that number is roughly one out of three (Greenwald, 2012). FG students differ in significant ways from their non-first-generation peers in areas that range from racial, ethnic, and socioeconomic demography to academic preparation, transition to college, and parental role in the college choice process. (Billson & Terry, 1982; Engle & Tinto, 2008; Horn & Nunez, 2000). Specifically, FG students are more likely to be students of color, nonnative English speakers, immigrants, single parents, and financially independent from their parents (Bui, 2002). They are less likely to have access to rigorous secondary curriculum, such as advanced placement classes, mathematics, and ACT or SAT preparation, and are overrepresented in developmental or remedial courses in college. (Bui, 2002; Engle & Tinto, 2008; Jehangir, 2010a). Finally, they are less likely to begin college at a four-year institution (Karen, 2002), carry a full-time credit load, or complete a bachelor's degree (Cabrera, Burkum, & La Nasa, 2003).

Yet, for many of these students, the promise of matriculation falls short (ACT, 2013; Adelman, 2007; Chen & Carroll, 2005; Engle & Tinto, 2008). Gaps in degree attainment and persistence for FG students are wide, with significantly fewer of them (27.4%) earning a degree after four years than students whose parents earned college degrees (42%; DeAngelo, Franke, Hurtado, Pryor, & Tran, 2011). This gap (14.7%) remains largely unchanged at the six-year mark, demonstrating that not only does the potential for college to serve as a medium for social mobility and equity remain unmet, but also that students may be leaving college with considerable debt and no degree.

In 2013, the Obama administration hosted a daylong summit attended by several hundred college presidents and focused on the role of educational access and success in fighting generational poverty (Tyre, 2014). The summit made clear that the success of low-income college students is tied to the country's larger issues of economic welfare, job preparedness, and civic engagement, and this issue is now a focal point of public discussions across educational, business, and community organizations (Baum, Ma, & Payea, 2010). It is clear that social class, race, and immigrant status are intertwined for many first-generation students. Thus, making good on the economic promises of higher education means attending to the needs of this population. A window of opportunity now exists for institutions to consider how their policies, practices, and politics need to change to more effectively serve all their students. This opportunity for changing institutional culture is coupled with an economic necessity to retain students, particularly as state funding has dwindled for higher education (Engle & O'Brien, 2007).

Previous literature on first-generation student persistence has considered multiple factors, such as lower GPA and ACT scores, parental income, English-language proficiency, and academic preparation for college. These issues all represent legitimate constraints to degree completion, but they can also serve to problematize the students themselves rather than explore the ways in which the academy has failed to adapt to this growing population of students (Engle, 2007; Engle & Tinto, 2008; Gibbons & Borders, 2010; Pascarella, Pierson, Wolniak, & Terenzini, 2004; Pike & Kuh, 2005; Ramos-Sanchez & Nichols, 2007). In addition, much attention has been given to the first-year experience of FG students because a significant portion of this population is not retained to the second year (Choy, 2001; Engle & Tinto, 2008; Jehangir, 2010a; Nuñez, 2011; Pascarella, 2004; Ward, Siegel, & Davenport, 2012).

The purpose of the study was two-fold: (a) to bring attention to the experience of low-income, FG students beyond the first-year and (b) to create space for these students to reflect back on their collegiate journey with the intent of capturing both the challenges they faced and the forms of agency they employed to persist. As such, participants were primarily junior and senior undergraduate students. Central to this report are the voices and narratives of predominantly low-income, FG college students—many of whom are immigrants or the children of recent immigrants. This demographic profile was intentional as we sought to reflect the growing diversity of FG students on campuses around the country. While most FG students begin college at a two-year institution, this study was set at a four-year institution. Thus, it provides important insights into educational experiences that facilitate or hinder baccalaureate degree completion but may offer limited understanding into two-year college experiences of FG students or the contexts that support transfer. Drawing on these student voices, the research and practice literature, and a theoretical framework described in the next section, this report considers institutional contexts with particular attention to FG students'

- demographics and multiple identities,

- postsecondary challenges and the dominant and nondominant means of capital they employed to navigate through college, and

- interactions with institutional agents (e.g., academic advisors, admissions representatives, student life staff, multicultural student support staff) that affect their college success.

The primary audience for this report is faculty members, staff, and administrators at four-year institutions. That said, the voices and contributions of the participants in this study add to our understanding of how educators and higher education professionals in a variety of institutional settings can best serve the first-generation student population.

First-Generation Students: Intersecting Contexts and Identities

Much has been written about the experiences of students who are first in their families to go to college. The term *first-generation* does not have a standard definition in the literature. Typically, it refers to students who are first in their immediate families to attend college, but how parental postsecondary experience has been defined varies. Billson and Terry (1982) defined FG status as having parents with no college experience. By contrast, federal TRIO programs for low-income and underrepresented students define FG students as individuals for whom neither parent completed a baccalaureate degree (U.S. Department of Education, n.d.). Within this report, FG students include those whose parents did not attend college or did not earn a four-year degree.

Research on FG students includes qualitative (e.g., Bryan & Simmon, 2009; Coffman, 2011; Hartig & Steigerwald, 2007) and quantitative studies (Chen & Carroll, 2005; Dennis, Phinney, & Chuateco, 2005; Dumais & Ward, 2010; Inkelas, Daver, Vogt, & Leonard, 2007; Ishitani, 2003) as well as personal narratives of working class and first-generation academics (Davis, 2010; Graham, 2011; Housel, 2011; Oldfield, 2012; Rendón, 1994; Vander Putten, 2001). To date, this literature base has largely identified constraints (e.g., GPA, parental income, ACT scores, English language proficiency, and academic preparation for college) that limit both matriculation and retention for FG students. While this research has been immensely helpful in understanding the forces that impact decision making about and progress in higher education, an opportunity exists to shift the discussion beyond student deficits to an examination of the strengths of FG students and strategies for capitalizing on these strengths.

This section begins with a brief overview of what we know about FG students and then extends the discussion to the multiple identities and contexts of these students, specifically

- What are the demographic intersections that make up the FG student population?
- How does this confluence of contextual and factors impact FG and immigrant college student success to and through college?

The theoretical framework that informed the study design and data analysis follows along with the major questions guiding the current study.

Multiple Identities and Complex Contexts

A profile of FG college students reveals them to be a heterogeneous group with regard to demographics, while simultaneously sharing many experiences that characterize their journey to and through college (Soria & Stebleton, 2012; Stebleton & Soria, 2012). FG students are more likely than their non-FG peers to be over the age of 24, female, low-income, students of color (particularly Black or Hispanic), and have a disability (Bui, 2002; Engle, 2007). They are also more likely to be nonnative speakers of English, single parents, and born outside the United States (Choy 2001; Engle & Tinto, 2008). In addition, they are employed (often full time) while enrolled in college to pay for personal and family expenses (Jehangir, 2010a; Soria & Stebleton, 2012; Stebleton & Soria, 2013). While not all students of color or low-income students are FG, the persistence data on these specific groups can help shed light on the FG population. For example, as recently as 2009, the six-year college graduation rates for African American, Hispanic, and Native American students at four-year institutions were 39%, 49%, and 38%, respectively, which lagged behind the rates for White (61%) and Asian/Pacific Islander (69%) students (Aud et al., 2011). A similar picture presents itself when considering the persistence gap between low-income students and their higher income peers. Engle and Tinto (2008) found that regardless of institution type, low-income, FG, college students "were nearly four times as likely to drop out of college after their first year, compared with their non-first generation peers" (p. 13).

Part of the challenge to better understanding this student group is acknowledging there has been "little cohesiveness in defining and examining these students experiences" (Walpole, 2007, p. 7). The following sections consider the confluence of demographics—such as family income level, social class, race, and immigrant status—that increasingly typify the experiences of students who are first in their families to go to college. The intent is to name the demographic intersections and to unpack how attention to these identities can influence our understanding of the lived experience of FG students.

Socioeconomic Status and Social Class

Research about FG students often intersects with literature examining the effects of socioeconomic status on college access and success (Beegle, 2000; Carnevale & Rose, 2004; Longwell-Grice & Longwell-Grice, 2007; Vander Putten, 2001). Beegle (2003) identified four types of poverty and low-income statuses among college students: (a) generational, (b) working-class, (c) immigrant, and (d) situational. She found that students coming from a generational poverty background often had little or no evidence of how someone in the community had benefitted from education, and education was frequently trumped by more pressing life issues. For poor working-class students, an oft-heard message was that their poverty was a form of personal deficiency. Beegle (2003) also noted that many immigrants experience poverty due to the circumstances of their arrival in the United States, where they may face language and cultural barriers and where previous educational experiences may no longer be valid. Finally, situational poverty refers to individuals who are in poverty for relatively shorter, but often recurring, periods of time as a result of a particular life event, such a chronic illness, job loss, or death in family.

Another factor influencing educational and career or life choices among FG students is social class. "While income often is considered to be synonymous with social class, in actuality social class is a combination of economic status, values, beliefs, attitudes, and assumptions" (Okun, Fried, & Okun as cited in Longwell-Grice & Longwell-Grice, 2007, p. 410). Jehangir (2010a) expanded on these definitions, noting "while income may be a numerical determining of one's financial worth, social class captures the nature of one's life experience, aspirations, and family expectations, said or unsaid, as shaped by income, work, domicile, and family history" (p. 15).

The literature on social class and educational experiences has taken up the issue in the following ways: attention to family income (Paulsen & St. John, 2002; Perna, 2005; Teranishi, Ceja, Antonio, Allen, & McDonough, 2004); parental education as a determinant of collegiate success (Choy, Horn, Nunez, & Chen, 2000); and parental occupation and impact on collegiate success (Marks, Turner, & Osborne, 2003; Tett, 2004). Between 1990 and 2010, immediate college enrollment of high school completers from low- and middle-income families was 52%, a full 30 percentage points lower than students from high-income families. The percentage of 12th graders who planned to attend college was also closely tied to parental degree attainment, where students whose parents had a bachelor's degree were significantly more likely to plan to graduate from a four-year institution (Aud et al., 2012). In addition, the impacts of social class, with regard to income and lifestyle, have a significant academic and psychosocial effect on the educational trajectory of young people (Barratt, 2011; Chatman, 2008). These influences may manifest themselves in different ways, including questioning one's self-efficacy and ability to succeed in college in light of the perception of more prepared peers, as well as experiencing social isolation in both the classroom and on campus. As such, there is increasing attention to expanding these discrete concepts of economic and educational categories to include the effect that class has on ideology, aspirations, and way of life, which in turn shape one's world view (Bourdieu, 1990; Walpole, 2007).

Further, while attention to income is critical to understanding educational mobility, the way in which income affects access to resources and perception of education is equally important. These distinctions in lived experience among low-income, FG students and majority students raise the issue of social and cultural capital (Bourdieu, 1977, 1990, 1994; Yosso, 2005). *Cultural capital* is a sociological term used to describe, "the tangible/intangible elements in society that provide advantages and disadvantages to certain individuals living in that society" (Madyun, Williams, McGee, & Milner, 2013). Resources may include items available in one's home ranging from books and computers to access to ACT preparation classes (e.g., tangible items) but also intangible resources, such as messages about of the role of education in one's life and access to individuals who might influence perceptions of college. *Social capital*, on the other hand, pertains to one's existing network of people and community and the extent to which these networks can create access to particular spaces and contexts.

Stuber (2011) contended that within educational contexts, social capital acts as an invisible resource with particular regard to knowledge and understanding about the nuances and expectations of collegiate culture. She argued further that within higher education, cultural capital and entitlement allow individuals from the dominant classes a heighted sense of comfort and savvy about negotiating the institution, primarily because the cultural norms of American higher education are predicated on middle- to upper-classes mores. As such, low-income, FG students who are unfamiliar with the social and cultural mores of collegiate life may experience isolation and anxiety, "making it difficult or even undesirable for such students to become integrated into the collegiate context" (Stuber, 2011, p. 119). Students' awareness that they lack the right social and cultural currency, coupled with limited connections to the larger campus community (i.e., instructors and classmates), can impact their sense of belonging and academic efficacy (Baumeister & Leary, 1995; Hoffman, Richmond, Morrow, & Salomone, 2003; Pittman & Richmond, 2007; Soria, & Stebleton, 2012).

To further understand the impact of social class on low-income, FG students in the academy, Stephens and colleagues (2012) suggested a theory of cultural mismatch, arguing that individual success is dependent on the extent to which students feel institutional norms and values coincide with their own. Their analysis of four different institutional contexts suggested a "critical factor underlying the social class achievement gap is American universities' focus on middle-class norms of independence as the culturally appropriate way to be a college student" (p. 1178). This notion of independence is often at odds with a culture of interdependence practiced by many FG and working-class students (Lamont, 2000).

Immigrant Status

Many FG students also have immigrant status, defined broadly to encompass first- and second-generation immigrants, including refugees born outside of the United States. As the immigrant group in the United States continues to grow—now at roughly 41 million (Nwosu, Batalova, & Auclair, 2014)—many are pursuing postsecondary education as a path to upward mobility. Based on Staklis and Horn's (2012) data from the National Center for Education Statistics (NCES), approximately 23% of all undergraduates are immigrants (i.e., foreign-born or second-generation Americans). Kim and Diaz (2013) and Gildersleeve (2010) highlighted a host of concerns among immigrant (and often FG) college populations, such as English-language proficiency, developmental education, documentation status, parental involvement and expectations, psychological development and acculturation (e.g., food, housing, clothing, transportation), separation from family members, social identity development issues, and career aspirations and life-career development issues. Given that 51% of participants in this study self-identified as immigrants, it was important to capture the complexities of this identity.

New immigration trends indicate a shift in ethnic backgrounds to include more people of color, an increased number of African immigrants (Roberts, 2014), and refugees entering the United States. Black Africans are currently one of the fastest growing immigrant populations in the United States, largely due to postcolonial conflicts and political instability in Africa (Thomas, 2011). Of the annual one million immigrants entering the United States, approximately 10% arrive from African countries, with almost half (47%) of this group emigrating since the year 2000. Presently, approximately 13% of all college-age Blacks in this country are the children of African, Caribbean, or West Indian immigrants, or are immigrants themselves (Kent, 2007). Minnesota, the geographic area of this study, is home to the largest population of Somali residents and has the ninth largest population of African immigrants, including Ethiopians, Liberians, Kenyans, and Nigerians, nationally (Remington, 2008). In the case of Minnesota, these newcomers and their children are changing the demographics of secondary school systems and aspire to college education. Further, since many of these Minnesotan immigrants, especially those with refugee status, have limited formal education, their children are often first in their family to attend college.

Race

As reflected in the 2010 U.S. Census Bureau report (2010a), the United States is undergoing a period of significant demographic shift, and while Whites still constitute the single largest racial group in the country, Hispanic and Asian populations have grown considerably, in part because of immigration. The latest projections from NCES suggest that between 2011 and 2022, elementary and postsecondary school will see the following increases in their students of color populations: Black 2%, Asian 20%, Hispanic 33%, and multiracial 44% (Hussar & Bailey, 2013). In addition, population projections suggest the United States will "become a majority-minority nation for the first time in 2043. While the non-Hispanic White population will remain the largest single group, no group will make up a majority" (U.S. Census Bureau, 2012, para. 11). These data reinforce earlier forecasts suggesting that the fastest growing segments of our population are young people from communities of color, many of whom are immigrants (Kelly, 2005; Kim, 2014; Mortenson, 2006a, 2006b).

As populations for communities of color and immigrants continue to grow it is also salient that these groups are disproportionately living in poverty. Aud et al. (2013) found, in 2011, 22% of all children under the age of 18 were in families living in poverty, with rates varying across racial and ethnic groups and highest for Black children (39%), followed by American Indian/Alaska Natives (36%), Hispanics (34%), Native Hawaiian/Pacific Islanders (30%), and children of two or more races (22%). The poverty rate was lowest for White (13%) and Asian (12%) children (Aud et al., 2013). It is important to note that while Asian students appear to be doing better than all other students, these data do not disaggregate Asian students into subgroups of recent immigrant and refugee populations who face many of the challenges experienced by other communities of color (Chang, 2011; Museus, 2011).

Thus, to talk about FG students often means considering race; income; social class; and, increasingly, immigrant identity and status (i.e., documented and undocumented). Given these demographic shifts, the academy needs to prepare for more students whose cultural, racial, and social-class identities may be vastly different from those who have traditionally come to college. Even as access to higher education has increased considerably for diverse FG students, Rendón, Jalomo, and Nora (2011) argued that "much more work needs to be done to uncover race, class, and gender issues (among others) that impact retention for diverse students in diverse institutions" (p. 244).

Demography and Lived Experience: Impacts on the Educational Journey

Engle and O'Brien (2007) stated that while demographics can impinge on educational outcomes, demography is not destiny if institutions are effective in understanding their FG population and translate that knowledge into policies and practices that support their persistence. The road to and through college is not a clear path for many FG students. The following sections seek to address how demographics impact the educational journey.

Aspirational Identities: Family and Community

When do young people begin to think about college, and how do they envision their educational future and their life trajectory? This question is at the core of how FG students and their families experience college, particularly in light of the variance in social and cultural norms between the academy and their enrolled FG students. The journey to college can be divided into three stages, according to Hossler and Galagher: "predisposition, preparation and matriculation" (as cited in Jehangir, 2010, p. 21). For FG students who are from low-income, immigrant communities of color, the process can be quite different than for non-FG students.

The first phase (predisposition) considers how family and community perceptions of education shape and communicate the importance and value of college. For some FG students, the educational milieu, especially postsecondary education, is a foreign idea and space that has little connection to the daily lives of people they know (Barratt, 2011; Howard & Levine 2004; Jehangir, 2010a; Rendón, 1992). Howard and Levine (2004) highlighted the alien nature of college in poor communities: "examples of success just don't exist in most poor communities, anymore … it's a world in which students are unaware of avenues out and in which parents haven't had a great deal of success with the educational system" (p. 20). Yet, as the value of a high school degree has declined in the job market, there has been a shift around predisposition to college, especially for FG immigrant students as reflected in their growing college matriculation numbers (Suárez-Orozco, Suárez-Orozco, & Todorova, 2008). Richardson and Skinner (1992) referred to this predisposition phase as "opportunity orientation" (p. 30), or the extent to which students have even considered college as part of their future. Often, FG students and their families have not carefully planned or discussed the possibilities of a college degree. As a result, they may begin planning for college later than peers. This late entry into the game impacts both preparation and matriculation to college.

The second phase (preparation) involves selecting and applying for college and financial aid. For continuing-generation students, parents often play a critical role in guiding them through this process, with everything ranging from college tours to filling out paper work and writing essays. For FG students, this same process can be overwhelming and lonely. Their parents are less likely to have experience with negotiating applications and the financial aid process. In addition, choosing a college may be influenced by familial roles that require proximity to home either for cultural reasons or because, even in college, these students continue to be a breadwinner for the family (Choy, 2001; McDonough, 1997, Terenzini et al., 1994).

The impact of parental education also bears out in matriculation (the third phase). While children of parents without college degrees are less likely to aspire to higher education, those who make it to college are twice as likely to leave without a degree (Choy, 2001). Failure to complete college is tied to a range of factors, including challenges adjusting to the institution while trying to stay connected to family and community, academic preparation, self-efficacy, financial constraints, and institutional effectiveness in supporting FG students.

College Transition

While all college students undergo a period of transition as they make sense of their new environment, the FG student may face unique challenges, such as how to explain this world to family members who have little context and understanding of the culture and expectations of academia (Oldfield, 2007, 2012; Pérez & McDonough, 2008; Rendón, 1996). FG students may also feel the push-pull of continuing to fulfill family obligations while balancing the new academic demands of college. These obligations can be tangible, ranging from caring for siblings, doing domestic chores, or being a cultural broker or translator between the family and external institutions (e.g., healthcare systems, government offices, schools). For parents who rely on their children's help to sustain the family unit, there can be a gap in understanding why the child who took on additional responsibilities in high school can no longer do so in college, despite a seemingly more open schedule of classes. Thus, while college is a time to focus on self and development for many non-FG students, FG students may find they do not have this opportunity.

Even more challenging might be negotiating the intangible expectations about career choice, the meaning of work, and questioning authority. Lareau's (2002) work on race and social-class differences among middle-class, working-class, and poor families suggests that different values guide parenting based on class. She found middle-class children tended to have more structured and extracurricular, activity-driven, home environments while working-class and poor children had more free time and focused on relationship building with family and friends. More recently, she noted that a key difference among middle-class, working-class, and poor families was their interactions with those in power (Lareau, 2011). Middle-class families placed more emphasis on networking with those in power (e.g., teachers, physicians) and were assertive in their exchanges with those in authority. By comparison, working-class and poor families were more likely to defer to those in power and less likely to question information presented to them. These findings suggest that low-income, FG students may have difficulty navigating not only the seemingly contradictory expectations of school and home but also educational environments that encourage contesting ideas and viewpoints. It is no surprise then that many FG students feel like imposters in academia and may lack confidence, especially in their first college year. This uncertainty about their place in higher education compounded with competing home, employment, and familial responsibilities can affect academic and social engagement, and, in turn, can negatively impact student success and, ultimately, persistence toward graduation. (Jensen, 2004; Megivern, 2003; Soria, Stebleton, & Huesman, 2013).

Collective Dreams and Expectations

For FG and immigrant students, college is the path to social mobility not only for themselves but for their entire families. Students may feel compelled to pursue degrees in areas that have the promise and prestige of certain careers (e.g., medicine, law, business) because of the financial stability they provide. As such, the path to upward mobility for the student and the parent may be significantly different (Deenanath, 2014). Many immigrant and low-income parents emphasized financial security over career fulfillment or interest (Dundes, Cho, & Kwak, 2009; Hodge & Mellin, 2010; Xie & Goyette, 2003) and have a specific career path in mind for their children, often related to the science, technology, engineering, and mathematics (STEM) fields. If students deviate from this path, there can be family dissonance (Lucas, Skokowski, & Ancis, 2000). Further, in many immigrant communities, there may be only a few professionals (e.g., doctors, dentists) serving as role models of upward mobility; this may narrow parents' frame of reference pertaining to how their child can succeed in the new world and limit the social and cultural capital of the student (Deenanath, 2014). Thus, FG and/or immigrant students can face the additional burden of trying to explain to their parents that they can achieve upward mobility through various avenues and be their own role models.

Financial Constraints

Postsecondary education is becoming a necessity in today's economy and may serve as a way to break the cycle of poverty for low-income families (Carnevale, Rose, & Cheah, 2011; Rothkopf, 2009). Yet, the rising costs of a college education are a significant concern for many students. According to National Survey of Student Engagement (NSSE, 2012) finances was a significant concern for many of the 15,000 first-year and seniors who completed the survey. Three in five first-year students and more than half of seniors were concerned about paying for college and regular expenses. The educational journey is further complicated for low-income, FG students who are also facing decreasing financial aid and assistance that is not keeping pace with college expenses (Engle & Tinto, 2008). For example, the federal needs-based Pell Grant covered 78% of the annual tuition for recipients at the program's inception in 1965, with this amount dropping to 37% within the past 40 years (Mumper, 2003).

For low-income, FG students and their families, navigating the financial aid system can also be daunting. Some might even opt-out of federal financial aid due to a lack of understanding of the process (Mumper, 2003). With fewer grants available, low-income students may be forced to take on loans to fund their education (Mumper, 2003), a situation further complicated by the fact that many low-income families have negative experiences with and are averse to taking on debt, thus introducing additional barriers to attending college (Burdman, 2005; Gudmunson & Danes, 2011). To alleviate the financial burden of paying for college, many of these students pursue part-to-full-time employment to lessen some of their fiscal burdens. The results of the 2012 NSSE concluded that although 60% of students who were employed believe working interferes with their academic performance, they would choose to increase the number of hours worked if it meant borrowing less. As such, the cost of financing a college education may negatively impact graduation on time or if at all (DeAngelo et al., 2011).

As FG students prepare to attend college, they must negotiate the complex web of financial issues, familial roles and expectations, and their own changing and emerging identities. To serve and support this group, higher education professionals need to better understand the multiple and fluid FG identities, which can become more salient and pressing in different milieus. To that end, this study sought to explore three questions:

- What can we learn from upper-division FG students about their perceived obstacles and support received throughout their enrollment at a four-year, predominantly White institution?

- What can we learn from these students whose accomplishments and engagement rendered them to be success stories, even if that is not how they may have described themselves?

- How might a deeper understanding of the complexity of these students' experiences through the college years—both positive and negative—inform policy, programmatic initiatives, and intersecting services on college campuses?

A discussion of the theoretical framework guiding our examination of these questions follows in the next section.

Theoretical Framework

Bronfenbrenner's developmental ecology theory (Bronfenbrenner, 1976, 1977, 1993, 1994, 2005; Bronfenbrenner & Morris, 2006) served as the guiding framework in exploring the context of the lived experience of the study participants. Although initially applied to the study of adolescent development and behavior, Bronfenbrenner's work has been extended to a wide range of populations and contexts, including college students and developmental theory (Evans, Forney, Guido, Patton, & Renn, 2010; Kim & Diaz, 2013; Stebleton, 2011).

As an ecological model, Bronfenbrenner's theory is part of a rich history in higher education literature of approaches to understanding college environments (Banning, 1978; Banning & Kaiser, 1974; Strange & Banning, 2000). Ecological methods examine the interaction between the person (i.e., the student) and the environment, with an emphasis on the processes involved—not the specific outputs or outcomes—as well as the fluidity of development in relation to salient events and interactions in students' lives. Evans and colleagues (2010) described ecological models as "integrative in the ways that they account for multifaceted contexts for the development of the whole student" (p. 159). They also offered insight into "how campus environments can be shaped to promote optimal growth and development" (p. 159). Renn and Arnold (2003) expanded on the importance of considering environmental factors by noting

> postsecondary educators need to understand the reciprocal interacting effects of various subenvironments, levels of environments, and students themselves. We also need to know which student characteristics relate to their degree and type of responsiveness to different environments. Above all, we need to specify the processes by which these interactions produce change in individuals. (p. 264)

The developmental ecology framework also has a constructivist perspective, addressing how realities are made and behavior is understood (Anzaldúa, 1999; Brott, 2005; Weber, 1998) and "assum[ing] that people, including researchers, construct the realities in which they participate" (Charmaz, 2006, p. 187). Moreover, a constructivist lens acknowledges the interactions between the person and the environment, as well as the shared meaning that students assign to certain events, processes, and interactions within a learning context (Baxter Magolda, 1999; Guido, Chávez, & Lincoln, 2010; Lewin, 1936).

Higher educational professionals have recently applied the developmental ecology framework to a variety of postsecondary contexts, including student affairs practices such as academic advising, college counseling, and mental health (Cerezo, O'Neil, & McWhirter, 2009; Stebleton, 2011). It has also been used to study the experiences of first-generation and/or immigrant college students. For example, Arana, Castañeda-Sound, Blanchard, and Aguilar (2011) conducted a study on Hispanic students and the factors that led to greater persistence at a Hispanic-serving institution. Using Bronfenbrenner's model as a theoretical lens, they found that context (i.e., the interaction between students' context and the university context) played a significant role in terms of persistence and that students who persisted were likely to mention their FG status as a motivating factor. In a study exploring the experiences of immigrant college students, Kim and Diaz (2013) proposed a social-ecological model, based on Bronfenbrenner's work and ecological systems theory, arguing that it provided "a theoretical lens through which reciprocal interactions between individuals and their environments are examined in the context of specific aspects of a student's life history, social and historical circumstances, culture, and time." (p. 27). Stebleton's (2011) work on immigrant students also applied Bronfenbrenner's ecological framework to academic advisors and other institutional agents who interact with these students.

Key Features of the Developmental Ecology Model

Bronfenbrenner argued for an integrated, systems-based approach to human development where multiple diverse factors in the environment impact the individual and vice versa. His theory (1977, 2005)—also known as the PPCT model—proposes four interrelated components: (a) process, (b) person, (c) context, and (d) time.

Process

According to Bronfenbrenner and Morris (2006), the process component involves various forms of interactions or appropriate challenges (*proximal processes*) between the individual and the environment over time (e.g., visiting a professor during office hours; taking advantage of a campus leadership opportunity; managing school and home responsibilities). A key attribute of Bronfenbrenner's theory is that if development is to occur, students must engage in increasingly complex situations, actions, and opportunities during their time as undergraduates. These processes can occur inside the classroom (i.e., academic engagement) or in out-of-class contexts (e.g., residence hall, multicultural student organizations, peer groups, intramural sports).

Person

Bronfenbrenner (1993) described the person component as encompassing *developmentally instigative characteristics*, such as behavioral, biological, cognitive, psychological, and emotional attributes, which the student possesses and that impact human interactions with others (e.g., awareness of nonverbal cues; self-confidence; race or ethnicity; culturally specific physical attire). More generally, Evans et al. (2010) indicated that an understanding of these characteristics allows higher education professionals to see beyond the more common student demographics that describe students both individually and collectively—a critical ability as student populations become more diverse.

Context

Within the PPCT model, context may be the most important concept. Bronfenbrenner (1977) described context as "the ecological environment … conceived topologically as a nested arrangement of structures, each contained within the next" (p. 514), and which is dynamic in nature. A Russian nesting doll is an apt analogy. With varying sized structures organized around a central core, in the PPCT system, the core is the individual, or student, and the successive levels, or contexts, emanate outward. Figure 1 presents an example of the ecologic model as applied to the experiences of immigrant students in the work of Kim and Diaz (2013). Within the context feature are four additional, interrelated, and somewhat overlapping, dimensions that further delineate the student experience: (a) microsystem, (b) mesosystem, (c) exosystem, and (d) macrosystem.

Microsystem: Moving out from the core, Bronfenbrenner (1977) defined the first level as "the complex of relations between the developing person and environment in an immediate setting containing that person (e.g., home, school, workplace, etc.)" (p. 514). For immigrant and/or FG college students, examples of key microsystems can include family support systems, academic and support services, peer groups, faculty interactions (both inside and outside the classroom), college classes, place of residence, work responsibilities (both paid and nonpaid roles), family and communal expectations and wishes, out-of-class social activities, and participation in high-impact educational practices. Renn (2003) purported that each student is unique, and as a result, assumes his or her own distinctive set of microsystems.

Mesosystem. According to Bronfenbrenner (1977), "a mesosystem comprises the interrelations among major settings containing the developing person at a particular point in his or her life" (p. 515); it is a collection of microsystems. For FG and immigrant college students, this could include interactions between peer groups; family, class and faculty dynamics; employment settings; and multicultural spaces on campus (e.g., student union, student organizations, advising offices). The bidirectional arrows in Figure 1 represent the relationships between microsystem units. An example of a change in the structure may be when a commuting FG student moves from home to a residence hall and the resulting transition issues.

Exosystem: The next level moving outward from the center is the exosystem, which Bronfenbrenner (1977) defined as an "extension of the mesosystem embracing other specific social structures, both formal and informal, that do not themselves contain the developing person but impinge upon or encompass the immediate setting in which that person is found" (p. 515). They include, among other structures, interactions in the workforce (e.g., employment), the neighborhood, mass media (e.g., online social media, multimedia messages, and images), government (e.g., immigration laws and policies, financial aid policies), higher education institutions (e.g., access policies, support services), the distribution of goods and services, communication and transportation facilities, and informal social networks.

Macrosystem: This is the broadest level defined as "overarching institutional patterns of the culture or subculture, such as the economic, social, educational, legal, and political systems, of which micro-, meso-, and exosystems are the concrete manifestations" (Bronfenbrenner, 1977, p. 515). Examples of macrosystem influences might include cultural, social, historical, and political events in the United States and the immigrant's home country; the culture of higher education in the United States, including student and family members' expectations of college; belief systems, such as religion, philosophy of education, ideologies, family rituals, customs, and cultural roles; overt and covert societal expectations and messages about occupation, gender roles, and lifestyle choices; and cultural understanding and interpretations of issues related to race, ethnicity, gender, sexuality, and identity.

Time

Time relates to significant events in a person's life and when these events occur (e.g., for students it could be time of graduation, marriage, or obtaining a green card). Also, time refers to events that impact student choices (e.g., major or career decision making). Examples of the impact of time influencing immigrant and FG students include when immigrant families settled in the United States; immigration and financial aid policies in place while attending college; family dynamics, such as birth of a sibling, separation of a parent, and financial and/or emotional family support; and world events occurring during the college years and their consequences (e.g., 9/11 and subsequent changes to immigration policies; economic recession and resulting cuts in financial aid and job reduction). Analyzing the time element for FG students can potentially lead to a greater understanding of how these events may affect their experience and development as college students.

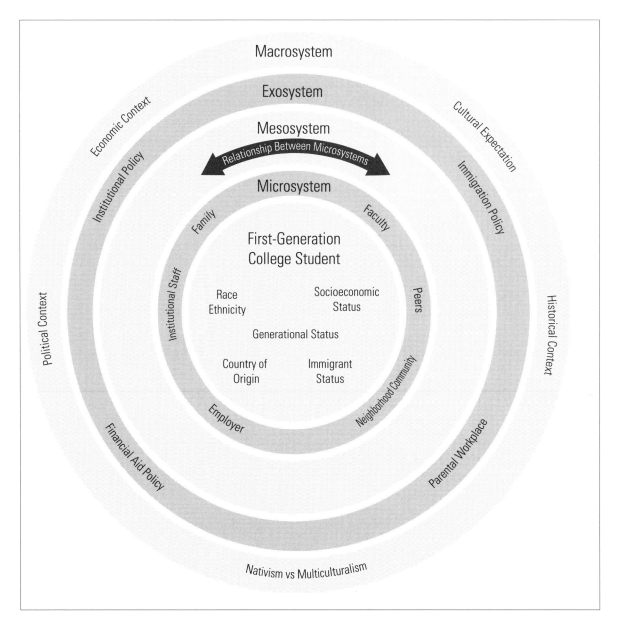

Figure 1. Bronfenbrenner's developmental ecology model. Adapted from *Immigrant Students and Higher Education* (ASHE Higher Education Report No. 38:6) by E. Kim and J. Diaz, 2013, p. 29. Copyright 2013 by The Association for the Study of Higher Education (ASHE).

Summary

Context matters and likely influences the experiences of FG and immigrant college students. From a systems framework, students interact with dimensions and factors within their environments, such as race, ethnicity, immigrant status, and socioeconomic status, which have the potential to shape identities and other aspects of college student development. Using Bronfenbrenner's ecological model, the remaining sections in this report explore how these personal factors can intersect across system levels (i.e., the immediate microsystem to distal exosystem) in the environment.

Setting the Context: The Focus-Group Study

This research report draws on data from a focus-group study conducted in the summer of 2011. The study sought to better understand the overall experience of low-income, FG, upper-division college students (i.e., juniors and seniors) at a large, public, predominantly White, midwestern, research institution. The term *predominantly White institution* (PWI) is commonly used to refer to institutions where more than 50% of the students enrolled are White (Brown & Dancy, 2010). At the time of data collection, the undergraduate enrollment at this PWI was as follows: 70% White, 9% international, 7% Asian, 4% African American, 2% Latino/a, 2% Native American, and 6% undisclosed. In the undergraduate class, 25% of all students received the federal Pell grant (University of Minnesota, n.d. - a). Within this cohort, 30% identified as first in their family to go to college. Among the FG students at this institution, 19% identified as students of color, with 86% of this group receiving financial support, including loans.

Methodology

Students were recruited via the TRIO programs and President's Emerging Scholars, a campuswide access initiative that also served low-income, FG students. The TRIO Student Support Services (SSS) program at University of Minnesota, funded since 1976, serves roughly 300 students annually. Approximately 83% of the students are from low-income families; 76% are both low-income and first-generation in college; 92% are students of color; 72% are nonnative English speakers; and 49% are foreign born. Student's low-income status was determined using two factors: (a) receipt of a Pell grant and/or (b) participation in a federal TRIO program. For the TRIO participants in this study, the average annual family income for a family of four was approximately $25,600.

An e-mail invitation was extended to students identified from these sources, and those interested responded to members of the research team to schedule a time to participate in the focus groups. The study includes data from nine focus groups ranging in size from four to eight participants, for a total of 39 students. The use of focus groups to collect data was particularly appropriate for this study since they provide an environment where "participants feel comfortable, respected, and free to give their opinion without being judged" (Krueger & Casey, 2009, p. 4).

Focus groups were designed to place students in subgroups reflecting common experiences, with particular attention to college of enrollment, FG and immigrant status, participation in TRIO or the McNair Scholars program (a TRIO summer undergraduate research initiative for low-income and underrepresented students), and involvement on the TRIO Student Board. While there was overlap among some of these categories, the intent was to create groups that differentiated between students' experiences in context of the programs in which they were involved and how these contexts shaped their perspectives and experiences during their undergraduate education.

Each session lasted approximately 90-120 minutes and followed the same format with attention to five core questions:

- What programs, services, experiences, or relationships have helped you succeed in college?

- What experiences made achieving these goals in college challenging?

- If you could create your ideal peer support group, given what you have experienced at the University of Minnesota in your courses and outside of the classroom, what would this group look like?

- What would make being a part of this peer support group attractive?

- What is one piece of advice you would give to University administrators or faculty to improve the college experience of students who are first in their family to go to college?

The group opened with an opportunity for participants to introduce themselves and write two or three words that captured their experiences as first in their family to attend college. Large-group discussion about these words and the feelings around them started the conversation, which then focused on the key questions. All sessions were audio recorded and transcribed verbatim. Prior to commencing the recording, researchers reviewed consent forms, and participants completed a brief demographic survey, self-identifying key categories (e.g., race, immigrant status, gender). Students received a $25 gift card at the conclusion of the group as compensation for their time.

Participants

Table 1 presents the demographics for the 39 study participants, who were primarily students of color (94%), female (62%), and immigrants (48%). Further, 85% received the federal Pell grant, typically awarded to students who have an estimated family contribution that places them in the lower quartile of family income in the United States (Heller, 2004). The sample comprised 26 juniors, 11 seniors, and 2 advanced sophomores.

Given the number of self-identified immigrants and students of color, the data demonstrate the intersection of identities between individuals who occupy and must negotiate multiple social spheres. While some researchers (e.g., Portes & Rumbaut, 2001) differentiate between first-, 1.5- (i.e., immigration before or during early teens), and second-generation immigrants, the participants in this study were only asked their country of origin and were not asked to report when their families arrived in the United States or documentation status. The entire sample was ethnically diverse; however, the majority of immigrants were from East Africa (67%) and Southeast Asia (33%). Immigrant students of East African ethnicity were primarily Somali refugees and immigrants from Ethiopia, Eritrea, and Sudan. Southeast Asian immigrants were from Thailand, and Vietnamese or Hmong refugees.

The Hmong students present a unique background since they are the only group whose cultural identity is not country specific (i.e., historical roots in China, Laos, Vietnam, and Thailand). Governed by 20 patrilineal clans (Donnelly, 1994), 89% of the Hmong population five years and older speaks Hmong in the home compared to 23% of the U.S. population who speak a language other than English at home (U.S. Census Bureau, 2010b).

Table 1
Participant's Demographic Characteristics (N = 39)

Characteristics	Freq.	%
Gender		
Male	15	38
Female	24	62
College status		
Sophomore	2	5
Junior	26	67
Senior	11	28
Race		
Black	23	58
White	2	5
Multiracial	4	10
Asian	8	20
Native American	2	5
Immigrant status		
No	19	49
Yes	20	51
If Yes, country of origin or cultural affiliation		
Ethiopia	2	-
Eritrea	2	-
Egypt	1	-
Sudan	1	-
Somalia	7	-
Thailand	1	-
Hmong	4	-
Pell Grant recipient		
No	6	15
Yes	33	85
TRIO participant		
No	11	23
Yes	28	72

Data Analysis

Interpretative narrative inquiry was used to capture and analyze the fullness of human experience through data collected in the form of stories (Clandinin & Connelly, 2000). This approach is well suited to research on deepening understanding of FG students' contexts and identities because stories capture the nuances and various frames, such as psychological, sociological, cultural, and familial (Hinchman & Hinchman, 1997). Further, focus groups include "social interaction in the construction of narratives" (Goodson & Gill, 2011, p. 5).

Maintaining the integrity and veracity of the student quotes, as shared in their own words, is of critical importance in qualitative research (Bernard, 1995). Keeping student quotes in their original form (e.g., using speaker's vernacular, dialect) provides a more authentic telling of the narrative and offers some context of the student experience as it relates to culture and environment. As such, very small edits to student data were made for clarity, with attention to maintaining the authenticity of the student voices.

The analytic process involved two separate phases. Initially, the three researchers who conducted the focus groups selected three of the nine sessions, and working independently, analyzed the data for meaning and potential emergent categories. The team then met collectively to draw on participants' text and create categories that surfaced within a single focus group. A cross-checking process (Flick, 1998) was initiated to develop categories that reflected the text across all three focus groups, concluding when no further categories were found. Finally, through a process of *categorical aggregation* (Lincoln & Guba, 1985), wherein overlap, differentiation, and saturation of themes were discussed, six meta-themes emerged: (a) Visible/Invisible, (b) Different Worlds, (c) Perpetual Border Crosser, (d) Burden of Privilege, (e) Establishing Voice, and (f) Call to Genuine Institutional Commitment. These are described in greater detail in the section that follows.

In the second phase of the analysis, the researchers first worked independently to assign codes reflecting the aforementioned themes to all text from all nine sessions. A new coder was included on the team who was not involved in creating the themes to determine the effectiveness, applicability, and validity of said themes. In addition, as is common in many qualitative approaches, this study sought to ensure trustworthiness of the data by engaging in an audit. Two researchers coded transcripts independently and then came together to discuss each code and confer on areas of disagreement. Using this discovery-based auditing approach, "each step in organizing the data involved a consensus process between the raters" (Yeh & Inman, 2007, p. 393). The consensus rate reflects strong interrater reliability. Of the 644 data points coded, raters were in agreement 88.86% and disagreed 11.14%.

Overview of Findings

All students in this study were low income and first in their family to go to college (i.e., first-generation). However, given that 51% of participants in this study were also immigrants, the data illuminate the heterogeneity in FG experience particularly as it relates to the intersecting identities of race, immigrant status, and social class. In some cases, both FG immigrant and nonimmigrant students experience similar barriers in the collegiate context. But the data also suggest points at which the immigrant FG students' experience might diverge from that of nonimmigrant FG students. Where the data give rise to issues that are particularly salient to immigrant FG students and their lived experience, this has been specified as such (e.g., refugee status, language, cultural context). When discussing implications, both groups (i.e., immigrant and nonimmigrant) are referred to while acknowledging that this FG population is diverse and heterogeneous. Thus, caution should be exercised in attempting to generalize these findings to other institutions or populations.

The six themes identified in the data analysis are (a) Visible/Invisible, (b) Different Worlds, (c) Perpetual Border Crosser, (d) Burden of Privilege, (e) Establishing Voice, and (f) Call for Genuine Commitment. Each theme captures different points of progression that participants articulated as they described their journey to and through college, ranging from an awareness or realization of their new realities particularly in the early part of their collegiate career to a movement toward negotiating, navigating, and finding agency in their multiple contexts. As reflected in Bronfenbrenner's theory, the components of process (forms of interactions or challenges); person (developmental characteristics); time (significant events in a person's life and when these events occur), and context are integral to the themes. While students' contexts (e.g., home, school, peers, work) remain constant, there is variance in students' developmental progression within each theme. Further, since the contexts they describe are unchanged, references to family, culture, school, and such are not relegated to any one theme but appear in each theme—the difference is how students negotiate these contexts and their identities in these contexts.

The first two themes—Visible/Invisible and Different Worlds—focus on students' transition to higher education. This transition was marked by struggle and an increasing awareness of the incompatibility of their contexts. Students expressed confusion and isolation about their place and identity at home, school, and the larger community. Visible/Invisible examines the FG students' contradictory experiences of being noticed or called out by faculty and peers while simultaneously feeling isolated in terms of terms of race, ethnic, religious, or class identity. Different Worlds captures the students' struggle between their old and new contexts (e.g., home, community, family vs. college, peers, work) and the frustration resulting from the increasingly incongruent expectations of these different spaces.

The next two themes—Perpetual Border Crosser and Burden of Privilege—examine the provocative moments in the students' home, school, and community lives that encouraged them to reflect, process, and explore ways to balance the incongruence they felt between their competing identities and the expectations of these different contexts. In the Perpetual Border Crosser theme, students share the ways they found to manage and become more facile at navigating their disparate worlds. Burden of Privilege expands on these negotiation strategies with students cultivating a space of interdependence, recognizing their deep responsibilities to their families while asserting their independence regarding career and life choices.

The final two themes—Establishing Voice and Call for Genuine Commitment—address resources, the role of staff and peer mentoring , and community engagement opportunities that moved students toward a greater sense of agency and belonging on campus. The themes focus on the impact that support and networking has on a student's ability to feel more adroit at crossing between multiple identities and contexts and to critique systemic constraints to his or her success. In Establishing Voice, students shared the networking, engagement, and leadership opportunities they found helpful in empowering them while creating a safe space of support within the academy. Call for Genuine Commitment offers students' pointed suggestions on how institutions and faculty could be more responsive to FG students in areas such as advising, mentoring, financial aid, institutional policies, and pedagogy.

While it is important to consider how each individual represents various facets of the FG experience, the data also revealed the six identified themes (Visible/Invisible, Different Worlds, Perpetual Border Crosser, Burden of Privilege, Establishing Voice, and Call for Genuine Commitment) are a representation of a process that participants engaged in from their early college years toward graduation. This process-oriented view of development, as defined by Bronfenbrenner's (1977) developmental ecology model, suggests connectivity between the themes. Across each theme, students noted arrival at a threshold of realization; engagement in self-reflection; and, in some cases, discomfort as they sought to balance their identities and contexts. This discomfort often served to propel participants to a place of better understanding and helped them embrace their multiple identities as FG students. An effort to consider how meaning-making interacts with the influences of context on the perceptions and salience of students' multiple social identities is also seen through these themes. This is most evident as and when students begin to travel from formulaic definitions of self to transitional self-understanding and toward a more foundational sense of personhood.

Through student narratives, the next three sections operationalize the theoretical framework in relation to the major findings of the focus-group study. The final section draws on the students' articulation of their adaptation process to discuss results, outline potential implications, and offer recommendations for strategies and promising practices.

Betwixt and Between: Visible/Invisible and Different Worlds

The two themes highlighted in this section—Visible/Invisible and Different Worlds—capture how participants expressed core struggles that typified their entry into the collegiate milieu and the disparities between how they sought to identify themselves versus others' (e.g., professors, peers, parents, extended family) perceptions of them. The components of Bronfenbrenner's model most applicable to these two themes are (a) microsystems (i.e., the collection of activities and interactions experienced by the student in their most immediate surroundings) and (b) mesosystems (i.e., the interactions between the student and the different environments). Visible/Invisible and Different Worlds demonstrate what FG students grappled with as they navigated their identities related to home, school, community, peer groups and employment, which were increasingly challenged by the incongruent expectations between these contexts. Awareness of the dissonance between their multiple identities is central to these themes while efforts to negotiate this dissonance remain a challenge for many students in this study.

Visible/Invisible

This theme refers to how FG students felt simultaneously visible (or called out) and also invisible on campus. A seemingly contradictory experience, it can be better understood with regard to how issues of race, class, and ethnicity were experienced in classrooms, around campus, and in interactions with faculty and peers. It is useful to note that of the five questions asked in the focus group, none were specific to race or ethnicity. Without any prompting, the students in this study commented extensively on how issues of race, ethnicity, and immigrant status intersected with their FG status. This underscores the complexity of the FG moniker by unearthing the multiple identities and cultural contexts that sit beneath it. The Visible/Invisible theme also represents how the FG students' transition to college has both overt and covert aspects. While feeling different, isolated, and even discriminated against because of race, religion, or ethnicity rendered them visible, their invisibility stemmed from an acute awareness that their lives and experiences were not reflected in campus life. They often lacked the social and cultural currency that seemed to open doors and create communities of belonging that were more easily accessible their non-FG peers.

Many students of color and immigrants felt their racial or ethnic identity was inferred by physical characteristics, such as clothing (e.g., head scarf or hijab) or accent. This visibility "othered" them and pushed certain aspects of their identity into greater salience in predominantly White spaces. Not surprisingly, students of color felt most visible and, as a result, lonely and isolated. Participants commented on becoming aware of the relative small number of students of color on campus. Mohamed, a Somali immigrant, student reflected on his orientation week:

> [The university] seemed diverse to me, but when we were in [the arena], and I was standing there and looking around, I couldn't believe what I was seeing … It was not very diverse at all. It was difficult to find like another Black person in the crowd.

This visibility was rendered more unnerving when students were faced with overt and covert expressions of racism. Tenzin, a multiracial immigrant student, reported overhearing racist comments muttered behind her in large lecture classes, where the absence of a critical mass of students of color seemed to create permission for students to make disparaging remarks:

> Other students, like in big lecture halls, they have no idea, but I have ears! I can hear you behind me saying these things. And walking around campus, going into a dorm someone yells out from their window horrible things [slurs]. One of my friends has a White friend who told her that he sees so many Asian people on campus, and he hates how they all walk around together, and he just wants to run them over with a car. … I'm just surprised there is still a lot of that.

FG students of color in this study were more likely to have attended diverse public, elementary and secondary schools, where interactions with a wide range of peers representing many different cultural, ethnic, and racial backgrounds can be commonplace. Several students felt their White high school peers where better equipped to cultivate multicultural friendships compared to their White college colleagues, demonstrating incongruence (i.e., regression) in their peer relationship mesosystems (i.e., interactions between high school and college experiences). Participants were surprised by the type of ignorance and racism they found on this campus, as noted by Janice, an African American student:

> I don't know how to say this. Coming to the University made me see racism in another way. I grew up with White people, and I used to hang out with White people and all that … people who are [used] to diversity and then coming here [to the University] with White people who have never seen … or gone to school with a Black person, you get to see the [amount] of ignorance there really is.

In addition to these overt expressions of racism, participants reported frequently feeling tokenized in class and forced to be representatives and ambassadors of their ethnic groups. They often felt pushed into isolating experiences not only by peers but also by faculty, who may be misguided on how to engage all students in the classroom. While non-FG students of color may also be called upon to serve a representatives of their race, this finding with regard to FG students who constitute a growing number of students of color demonstrates how race and class intersections created layered experiences that can undermine those who lack tools (cultural capital) or familial resources (social capital) to explain or contend with such aggressions. As such, classroom interactions could render a student highly visible but also voiceless, vulnerable, and invisible at the same time.

Participants reflected on the new awareness of this forced binary identity that thrust certain aspects of their personhood (e.g., race, nationality, language) to the center of their experiences. Kaja, an African American student, shared her experience within her major:

> In our major, we kind of focus a lot on how to work with African American kids, how to work with Latino kids … At first, it was like OK, maybe I am going to learn something new, but then after a while, you become the token *blackie* of the class. Somebody had the nerve to ask me, "How do you work with Black kids?" Same way you work with any other kid … the audacity of a person coming up to you and saying certain things. It's like, you just feel so overwhelmed with it, you feel so isolated, you can't really go to your teachers 'cause they are the ones who are teaching it, so it's like who do I go to?

This created a tension for students trying to articulate their multiple self-identities to various audiences in the college context. On one hand, participants relied on formulaic ways of describing themselves and their uniqueness (e.g., Latina, Black, Asian) while realizing the limitations of this binary view of self. This led to a desire to find people and contexts where their multiple identities could be understood. Olga, a multiracial immigrant student, commented on this tension:

> I mean, how I identify myself is unique. My dad is Mexican and my mom is Korean … that's unique in itself. I resonate more with my Latino side, 'cause I can speak the language. I majored in Chicano studies. … There are not very many Latino people on campus. There are not a lot of Latino professors. I just met the first one in the area that I am interested in—public health—this last semester, and that was my [last] year here. So just finding someone that you can get along with, someone you can have that personal connection with, and, like you know, [someone who says] I have been there, I kind of understand what you are going through.

Students reflected this same kind of invisibility and questioned their place on campus with regard to issues of social class and how effectively their teachers, schools, or family prepared them for college compared to other more privileged peers who came from college-educated families. Muna, a Somali immigrant student, shared her anxieties about measuring up to her peers and found herself wondering if she was up to the task:

> It was really hard for me to find people that looked like me. I was scared of what the classes would look like. I came from a public school, and I would look around, and I would know that half of those students were in private schools. They have a better education than I do; they come from better families, so it was really intimidating. I didn't know if I could be as good as they were. I didn't know [if] the work that I did was as good as their work.

Muna's comment highlights the duality of the Visible/Invisible theme in that she notes that her status as a person of color makes her visible but also simultaneously questions her academic ability to compete with other students in the class. Here, she is referring to her perception that many of her peers went to private schools, which reflected their higher social class, and worries that her public school education and lack of cultural capital will not measure up. This notion of measuring up and proving oneself as worthy peers of more affluent students is also reflected in an increasing realization that, in most cases, the families of FG students are not as well equipped to prepare their children for what to expect in college. Students regularly commented on working one or more jobs and feeling like the stereotypical portrait of campus life (i.e., going to class, playing Frisbee on the lawn) did not match their reality. In many cases, the actual experience of being simultaneously visible and invisible reflects the identity dilemmas and self-doubt that are at the core of the FG student experience.

Janice, an African American student, reflected on the constant struggle of wearing a mask to appropriately represent her community while also feeling like she must then hide or temper her true identity:

> That kind of loneliness and separation and always having to prove yourself to somebody, I feel like that's what we feel all the time on this campus, no matter what kind of courses we take. Even just walking around the mall … you don't want to talk too loud or seem ghetto … we are getting judged on everything we do.

Janice's comments speak to the intersection of race and social class that is part of the lived experience of so many FG students, raising the question, Who am I in this world, and where do I fit in?

Another example of this identity crisis is from Olga, a multiracial immigrant student whose experience demonstrates the push-pull on these students' multiple identities:

> It's like that whole identity piece is always challenged. I feel like you never really get to the bottom of it. I want to know when am I going to be like OK, this is it, this is me … and everybody is going to understand it's me. I am not representing this big group of people; I'm not my last name; I am *me* right now. I feel like that might never happen.

Olga's words captured both an increasing awareness of the incongruence between her multiple identities and the movement toward recognizing the relative salience of one identity over the other in various contexts. In recognizing the dynamic nature of her multiple identities, she expressed a need to name and define herself more effectively, and this recognition is a critical step in negotiating competing expectations within her microsystems. This identity dilemma is exacerbated by the chasm that FG students must often cross between their school world and the many circles of their home life (e.g., parents, siblings, extended community and home friends). For many students the realization that different aspects of identities have centrality in different contexts was integral in negotiating their different worlds.

Different Worlds

The nature of these challenges is addressed in the Different Worlds theme, which epitomizes the struggle between the old (i.e., home, community, and family) and the new contexts (i.e., the college environment, jobs, internships, clubs) students must navigate. Yet, this struggle is not binary. The nature of the home (old) world is complex and includes varying expectations, familial and cultural, coupled with financial issues, and a forced independence that comes from having to break with familial, cultural, and communal ways of knowing and being. As is typical of adult development processes (Hoare, 2006; Merriam, Caffarella, & Baumgartner, 2007; Tisdell & Swartz, 2011), entry into college results in a re-examination of identity, interests, goals, and expectations for most students. The difference for these FG students pertained to how they struggled to find belonging and balance emerging expectations and interests with familial hopes and demands.

Rendón (1996) called individuals who continually traverse different contexts in order to meet multiple demands (e.g., expectations of parents who do not fully comprehend the college experience) *border crossers* or *fronterizas*. As fronterizas become increasingly aware of the dissonance between their worlds, they must also make meaning of these incongruences. In the home context, the FG students in this study were starting to break away from their families, and as they changed in college, they felt they no longer fit in their home environment. Yet, students did not feel like they belonged in the academy either; their experiences were not validated, and they struggled to fit in. Straddling both worlds and the varying expectations of these spaces often resulted in a lack of belonging in either location.

While students were acutely aware of the pride their parents felt in their admission to college, they also felt increasingly isolated in their familial and community circles. At the most basic level was the feeling that their parents simply did not understand their new realities. Ranging from the heightened demands of academic work, to choosing a major, or balancing assignments for multiple classes, many FG students reported their collegiate experience was so alien to their parents that it was difficult to explain the facets of their new lives. In essence, it felt like they were speaking two different languages. Janice, an African American student, described this growing chasm with sadness and even some guilt:

> There are other things, just things they don't understand 'cause they haven't lived that life, so it's hard to make that connection with them because they have no background in it. I feel bad because I can't make that connection with them. Like, since you don't go to college, you don't understand what I am feeling. I don't want to say that because that's negative to say to somebody. It's not their fault they didn't get that chance, and that's just like a barrier I feel with our relationship as parent and child.

Many students expressed a realization that the increasing divide they felt from their families would likely continue to grow. They described a sense of impending loss and attributed it to the ways in which college pushed them upward in terms of social mobility but also away from their families, demonstrating again the conflict between the microsystems of the college and home worlds. Sierra, a multiracial student, described this isolation that stemmed from the increasingly different ways that she and her loved ones thought about the world, and the resulting separation:

> Like, my aunt, she is who I think of as my mother. She never went to college, and sometimes I try
> to reconnect, and I almost feel separate, like isolated from someone who I feel I should be really,
> really connected with. But it's hard to have conversations about things that matter to me now that
> would have never mattered to me if I didn't go to college. So, that was what I meant, it's almost as
> if it pushes you up, but then it takes you further away from people who you want to connect with.

The increased demands of academic work, coupled with employment and new social relationships, resulted in situations where FG students were struggling (sometimes with frustration and even anger) to explain and legitimize their new collegiate life to their families. In many cases, the inability to bridge the gaps between home, family, siblings, new friendships, ideas, and demands at college resulted in a sense of separation or distance from family. James, an African American student, described this increasing separation:

> I have had major detachment from my family, and mostly because I feel like they don't understand
> what I go through. My day is *not* lounge on the couch, go to class, and then go back and lounge on
> the couch. So, I get a lot of nagging about not being places. There are a lot of family functions that
> I miss out on because I am sitting at home writing a paper or reading a book.

At the core of these challenges was not only the family's limited understanding of the college experience, but also their continual comparison of high school contexts to college (e.g., schedule, academic rigor, expectations). Many students wrestled with trying to explain the structure or purpose of college to parents and siblings, differentiating between secondary and postsecondary experiences with mixed outcomes, at best. Abdi, a Somali immigrant student, reflected on his efforts to bridge this gap:

> I still see [my brother] look at me differently even though I explain it, "This is the reason why I
> do this," and you know I am trying to get into the system, trying to change myself. They go "Yes,
> Yes, Yes," but they don't *really* understand it, even though they listen, they don't really understand
> what it means.

This situation becomes even more complex given Abdi's status as an immigrant student. His parents may have had familiarity with the school system in his home country, but likely knew little about the transition from secondary to postsecondary education in the United States. In many cases, FG immigrant students report that their parents compare their progression in college to higher education in their home countries where access to professional training or medical school may occur at different points than in the U.S. system. For immigrant FG students, parents may not understand how the education system in their countries of origin and the United States differ, causing additional stress and misunderstanding between the parent and student.

As such, FG students experienced this feeling of isolation at college, with family and home community in both explicit and unspoken ways. For many parents, pride about their child's entry to college was coupled with the belief they had now arrived and were undoubtedly well equipped for college course work. After all, they had excelled in high school, and this expectation followed into college. Yet, being FG means these students are navigating the college process without the guidance of their parents.

Parents wanted their children to be successful and used the same mechanisms of support as they did when their student was in high school. Constant pressure to do well in school as representatives of their family and community only added to the students' level of stress. In many cases, these pressures to do well were directly linked to expectations to emerge from college with a specific career or vocation. Parents expected students to choose from a few select career paths that were tied to upward financial mobility or held the clear promise of a job. Overall, parents had limited knowledge about the links between college majors and career paths and tended to direct their children toward science, technology, engineering and mathematics (STEM) fields, favoring medical careers. Parents did not understand how the demands of collegiate work differed from secondary education and had a hard time accepting why their child may not be able to gain entry into a highly competitive major. Samir, an Egyptian immigrant student, explained the pressure he felt from his family:

> After my first year, they expected me to be a doctor right away … I was so shocked! [Becoming a doctor] was really hard for me, so I tried to talk to them. My dad … underst[ood], but my mom [did] not. So, I had to explain to her and bring it down to her … level.

These familial expectations were also often in direct contrast to collegiate expectations, where major and career exploration was encouraged by advisors, and students were being guided to consider strengths and interest-based inventories to determine future careers. Thus, students often felt caught between familial and educational units in the microsystem, trying to explain one to the other and determining how to balance these expectations. The time component of PPCT model is reflected in these situations where the environment and the interactions between student and family change over time due to shifting interactions within the system (Bronfenbrenner, 1994).

For FG students of immigrant parents, the pressure to be a role model within the family and community was especially intense. Many students reported that for immigrant parents, their children's success, relative to others in the community, was a source of great pride. Achieving good grades and pursuing career paths that were perceived as prestigious and lucrative elevated the family's social standing, while poor grades or choices that appeared to challenge parental expectations reduced family stature in the community. The comments of Nini, a Sudanese immigrant, reflect the respect for family and the fear of disappointing her parents, and by extension her community:

> I don't know what it is about my culture, but family is a pretty important thing … If you are going against what the family is saying, like my older brother, [you] got a lot of flak for it. You have these opportunities, and my parents were really upset 'cause they're refugees, like, they came all the way over here just so we could get an education.

Although parents counted on students to be high achievers in college, family obligations and responsibilities are still prevalent. Students were expected to go to college, come home, and complete chores. In many cases, these expectations were gendered, especially in immigrant families where the chores of cooking and care for young siblings often fell on female students (Chung, 2001; Phinney & Flores, 2002; Xiong, Eliason, Detzner, & Cleveland, 2005; Xiong & Huang, 2011). The expectations to be successful in college frequently did not match the reality of everyday life. Tee, a Hmong student, discussed this dilemma in her family:

> I came from a family of 10, and, throughout my first year, I couldn't live in the dorms because my parents are very traditional. And I am a female, so they said it's not good for me to live in the dorm. I had to come back home every day to clean and cook. My parents think college is so easy, they say stuff like "Oh it's so easy, if I went to college, I would be better than you."

Financial constraints compound the challenges faced by participants in this study, most of whom were from low-income families and expected to maintain multiple jobs, at times, to support themselves; their immediate family; and, sometimes, family abroad. Working was not a choice; it was a necessity. Olga, a multiracial immigrant student, and Sabra, a Somali immigrant, underscore these responsibilities:

> [Since] high school and throughout college, I have worked 2-3 jobs. That's normal for me … I mean, so not only am I a student, but I am a provider for my whole family. And then being part of that, not living on campus at all during the time I was an undergrad, took away from my experience, *my* college experience.—Olga

> Well, like for me, I have a lot of family back in Ethiopia that I am actually financially responsible for, so I help them … aside from like taking my full load of courses, and being involved in campus.—Sabra

Most FG students were cognizant of the delicate balancing act required to earn enough to support the family but not too much to jeopardize a financial aid package, which is based on family income. For many, the student pays the Expected Family Contribution (EFC) as defined by the Free Application for Federal Student Aid (FAFSA) because their parents do not have the means to do so. Hamza, a Somali immigrant, explained this dilemma:

> Yeah. It's so tough, but I have to like really work, and I have to support myself and my family through my part-time jobs. And at the same time, I have to watch out if I'm going to get financial aid, or any loans or scholarships. I mean, yeah, it's kind of tough, keeping that line not crossed.

The challenges related to employment and financial aid typify the struggles FG students have as they acknowledge, manage, and negotiate the demands of their different words. These dilemmas reflect how the FG students must make sense of and negotiate the interactions between exosystem (i.e., financial policies) and macrosystem (i.e., an economic reality over which they have little control) factors and their familial and collegiate experience. Increasingly, these students became aware that they would need external resources of support to thrive or even survive the college experience. Yet, for some FG students, the process of seeking help caused anxiety and feelings of being a failure. In many immigrant families and some communities of color, the expectation is that problems are resolved within the household and not aired publicly (Brilliant, 2000). Thus, seeking help can be incongruent with students' values and beliefs. Tina, a Thai immigrant, expressed her challenges with seeking resources:

> In the beginning, it was hard for me … I think that something freshman students need to know is to learn how to use our resources and [how to] look for resources. I come from a family where you try your best to do what you can without asking for help and that was the state of mind that I had. So I had to break myself out of the habit and relearn how to, you know, ask for help and things.

As FG students reflected on their journey through college, they wrestled with how to bridge the gaps between the different worlds: school and home, and new college friends and their social circle in the community. At the center of these challenges were competing ideologies. Families perceived college as a means to an end—financial security and a life better than the generation before. As such, choices for majors were often expected to be rooted in job opportunities and earning potential rather than a reflection on a student's exploration of interests. Yet, for many students in this study, the U.S. collegiate experience invited questioning and exploration of self, systems, and individual preferences that often competed with the goals and intentions of their home world or cultural context where job security, expediency toward degree completion, and certain careers are prized as pathways to social mobility. In addition, what they learned sometimes pushed them further from their families simply because both parties felt misunderstood, or worse, undermined. Also, at play was an individual versus collective approach to life planning. For many students, their successes were not individual but part of a larger family and community system. Yet, in the college environment, they were encouraged to think differently about their individual choices and path. This was confusing and challenging as Yang, a Hmong immigrant, notes:

> I didn't have a path to follow, and so the challenge in that is kind of finding my own path … where do I want to go, how does it work, and thinking about [my own] unique situation—that was a challenge for me.

Summary

The two themes discussed in this section positioned the FG student in contexts where they felt like they had little control or choice over how they were perceived. In the Visible/Invisible theme, FG students became increasingly aware of their multiple identities, particularly with regard to race; language; and, on occasion, religion or national origin (as denoted by external markers of color or perceived accent). Yet, these identities were defined *for* them—not *by* them. They were at times highly visible and called on to be representatives of their community or ethnic group, or, worse, subject to covert and overt racism and discrimination. At other times, they were rendered invisible by peers or faculty because they were pigeonholed into categories that were limiting at best. This invisibility extended to the ways in which their experiences as college students often did not match those of their peers and left them feeling like impostors in both academic and social realms. The sense of not knowing where to go, who to talk to, and what to ask—about everything from issues of discrimination to filing financial aid forms—underscored this invisibility. Jehangir (2010a) has likened this invisibility to being lost in an "alien landscape, while simultaneously figuring out rules and expectations, both implicit and explicit, which shape every facet of the college experience" (p. 30), all without the guidebook that other students seem to have.

To look at these themes side by side is to see how some of these challenges extended, ironically, into the home and family world as well. While there was support, pride, and love at home, here again, students felt like they were representatives of their community, role models, and standard bearers. In addition, they could not ask for the type of support they needed to grapple with the complex issues of college adjustment, whether this related to procedure and protocol or exploring majors, because their parents and community did not have the answers. As such, the Visible/Invisible and Different Worlds themes captured how many FG students are challenged on multiple fronts as they enter college and seek to find their way. These experiences raised questions and dilemmas pushing many FG students to explore ways to manage multiple roles, identities and aspects of their college experiences and respective cultures—a concept Bhabha (1994) labeled *hybridity*. Predominantly juniors and seniors, several students in this study began to articulate the processes by which they sought to challenge the dissonance they experienced and succeed in college on their own terms, as reflected in the next two themes.

Negotiating New Terrains: Perpetual Border Crosser and Burden of Privilege

The themes Perpetual Border Crosser and Burden of Privilege highlight students' realization that they must find ways to negotiate the disparate demands and expectations of their multiple worlds and context. These themes capture both an articulation of internal reflection as well as external actions that students undertook to try to mitigate the gaps between their different worlds and multiple identities. From the perspective of the ecological model, students were increasingly conscious of the mesosystems—points of interactions between dimensions of their microsystems (e.g., family, peers, classes, student-faculty interactions) as well as conflicts in these interactions. They also noted the way the exosystem (e.g., policies, practices) and macrosystem (e.g., culture, societal expectations, history) impacted how effectively they negotiated the gaps between their worlds. Based on navigating these complex systems, students learned what worked for them and began to practice negotiating their identities in different social contexts.

Perpetual Border Crosser

As noted earlier, FG students are not a homogenous group; they are constantly negotiating multiple worlds and identities, including, but not limited to, racial identity, gender roles, cultural and familial expectations, academic labels, and issues of social class and community. The theme Perpetual Border Crosser addresses how students in this study began to find ways to balance and juggle these many selves. The theme captures the challenges of navigating acculturation to college while trying not to give away one's old self in its entirety. Many students evoke the metaphor of border crossing (Rendón, 1996) and the feelings of loss and confusion this process gave rise to. In contrast to the Different Worlds theme, which focused on students' frustration with the incompatible expectations of multiple contexts, this theme highlights how they start to articulate a realization that managing this dissonance is important to their success.

A significant component of the transition to college and balancing the often competing expectations of home and school worlds involved naming these challenges. FG students across racial, ethnic, and immigrant groups commented on the emerging realization that entry into college and the experiences they were having on campus and in the classroom had little context in the lives of their family and friends. Shannon, an African American student, noted the inability to talk about school related issues in her community:

> I find that trying to speak with my family, or even long-time friends that didn't end up going to college … and converse with them about the things that I'm learning … like, there was just a barrier there. They just didn't know what I was talking about, and so that would become discouraging because I would want them [to] be excited about what I'm doing, but you can't really have a full-on conversation about it if they're not able to relate [to] what you're saying.

Her comments pinpoint the source of her frustration but also acknowledge that perhaps she must begin to adjust her expectations of her family and accept that there will be some aspects of herself and her development that she will simply not be able to share with her family.

Abdi, a Somali immigrant, unpacks this further by acknowledging that FG students cannot and do not want their families to be something other than what they are. There is a deep respect for the cultural traditions and familial support received, yet college was creating new questions, ideas, and identities for these students:

> Yeah, you can't tell your family to change, and when you are going through that, they think you are assimilating. Like … you are dissing your own culture, or who you are … So, it's a little different, and … it comes with its own problems.

Abdi's comments demonstrate that while his contexts stay the same, he is changing and must find ways to cross back and forth between his new identity as a college student and his life with his family. The pride he feels for his family and community is tinged with a sense of loss, an acknowledgement that perhaps he cannot be fully part of his old life and in turn his family cannot fully be part of his new life.

Tina, a Thai immigrant student, builds on Abdi's statement and noted how challenged she felt by naming her family as a stressor to her transition to college. Her comment demonstrates the central role of families in the cultural context of many FG students, particularly immigrant students, and how difficult it is to go against their wishes. Tina's experience reflects the dilemmas she faced as her microsystems of family and college seem to contest each other:

> That's what they teach you in my family, like, there's nothing more important than your family. So, then what happens when your problem *is* your family, like, they have [a] problem with you? Where do you go to? Who do you go to? So in a way, I just knew I had to … talk to someone about this, and I can't talk to them about it.

It is important to consider how the theme of Perpetual Border Crosser is situated against the both the themes of Visible/Invisible and Different Worlds. Each reflects a sense of isolation that students feel in changing locations and context between home and higher education settings and how these contexts affects whether students felt visible or invisible. However, in the Perpetual Border Crosser theme, students noted this increased awareness of forced binary selves resulted in being what Janice, an African American student, notes are "two different people … [with] … two fighting heads within yourself, so you are trying to know what side to show to who." Finding themselves in this position of discomfort pushed many students to begin thinking about how they might become more facile journeying between their worlds and identities. This process is reflective of increased meaning-making capacity as students negotiated the shifting relationship between context and salience of their identity dimensions (e.g., race, culture, class) and the understanding of their core identities. In many cases, students talked about how it was not just their transition but their families' transition as well. Abdi, a Somali immigrant, acknowledged the challenges of bringing his family along in a process that he himself was new to, underscoring the absence of a college navigator for FG college students:

> For me … there [are] two different cultures. When it comes to school there is a different culture. When I come to home, there is a different culture, and if you are going to college, you want your whole family to change theirselves, or adjust to the changes you are going through. … It's like someone who [goes on a] diet, the whole family has to go [on a] diet. You need that kind of support, that shifts from the family. It's very hard to do that.

Despite these challenges, many students talked about their effort to go the distance, while also trying to bring their family into their realities. Kim, an Asian American student, describes below how she felt the transition was not just about the college experience but also about being in a world vastly different from that of her parents. Consistent with familial and communally minded cultural frames (Xiong, Detzner, & Rettig, 2001; Xiong, Eliason, Detzner, & Cleveland, 2005), Kim is focused on not leaving her family members behind and helping them transition to this new world:

> I'm trying to help [my parents] understand. But it's hard for them to understand me since, you know, I'm going to school. I understand what's going on in the world, while they are still kind of stuck in their own traditional kind of thinking. … To [help my parents] to understand that there's steps that you have to go through to make it to where you want … that's kind of the challenging part of it.

Her attempts to slowly alter her family's perception not only makes the process of navigation easier for her but it may also smooth the way for younger siblings who might aspire to a college education.

Both Abdi and Kim note their efforts to engage their families in their new realities was very hard to do because their parents and siblings have no experience in the college context. The theme of Perpetual Border Crosser demonstrates how the student is changing even as old environments (e.g., home, family, culture) stay the same.

May Lor, a Hmong immigrant student, addressed the push-pull between honoring family and finding her own way. She noted that while college was her "chance to be independent, I also know that I shouldn't disappoint my family, at the same time." Mariah, an Asian American student, speaks to this constant fear of disappointing family while realizing she needed to make some of her own decisions:

> My first year going to college, I became more independent. I wanted to join in after school clubs and a lot of social things on campus, and my parents didn't understand what [that] kind of stuff [was]. They were disappointed, and you don't want them to be disappointed, but you keep trying, and you keep striving and trying to make them not disappointed. But you know, that [sense of] independence comes in and you have to do stuff on your own, which makes things difficult.

Mariah is cognizant to the internal struggle of wanting to keep her parents happy, yet, at the same time, maintain her independence; she is cognizant of the conflict. Additionally, May Lor and Mariah's comments reflect how a student's gender impacts their notion of independence, particularly for immigrant women. These students often reported greater constraints on participation in extracurricular or volunteer opportunities in college because their parents were concerned or fearful about their safety or felt these types of activities were not suitable for young women.

For students in this study, border crossing was not limited to navigating the distance between school and home. Students also needed to learn how to bridge the gaps among their own multiple identities (i.e., gender, race, and culture) even as the salience of these identities was constantly shifting.

Some students felt the campus support structures designed around identity labels did not cultivate spaces or invite dialogue across the national, racial, cultural, language, and geographic diasporas reflected in their lives. Rather, they felt pressured to choose one identity that would be their "home" identity on campus. Some students discussed experiences at student cultural centers and unions, noting they often felt torn and unable to fit in. Janice, an African American student; Melat, an Eritrean immigrant; and Chris, a Native American student, described the challenges they faced in various student organizations intended to support them:

> Oh, my dad is from Ghana, and my mom is Black American. In [high] school I just identified with Black, but coming here everybody is like, "Your last name is ___ that's not Black, what are you?" The African student groups they … don't work with me a lot because I don't speak Twi. I have never been back to Ghana, but I'm still of African [descent] but then Black people here say, "You are a half-erican," like you are half Black, so yeah, I'm always on both sides … and after my first-year … I didn't mess with Black Student Union at all.—Janice

> I don't like [to] participate, I support them … I would go to their events and stuff, but I could never *be* in those kind of groups. I tried, you know, to go join, but it's just, there's just something about me, I just don't feel like I'm only Ethiopian, or I'm only a Eritrean. I feel like I get challenged with that stuff.—Melat

> I will not go into the American Indian Cultural Center … I will not go in there. … being adopted, they don't like that.—Chris

In the Visible/Invisible and Different Worlds themes, students expressed frustration, surprise, and loneliness with regard to the incongruence and distance between their context and identities. In contrast, in Perpetual Border Crosser, they are in a process of accepting that they may not belong to any world completely and need to learn to navigate multiple spaces. There is an increased realization that their system(s) is not changing—they are changing. To be a perpetual border crosser is to be constantly conscious of the negotiation between multiple identities and contexts and trying to become facile with these transitions.

The metaphor of a bridge was repeatedly featured in students' dialogue around balancing the spheres of home, school, community, family, and peer worlds, as well as their efforts to find a new place between these seemingly disparate systems. Their awareness of the dilemmas of shifting identities in different contexts reflected how often they faced increasingly complex environmental factors that challenged them to think more deeply about how they wanted to identify themselves—and when and if they had that choice (Bronfenbrenner, 2005). The two comments below reflect the wide range of contexts these students engage in when grappling with identity issues. Hamza, a Somali immigrant, articulates the pressure and instability of balancing his identities as an immigrant and his growing sense of self, while Sierra, a multiracial student, questions when and if she would arrive at a more defined sense of self given her multiracial and queer identity:

> I am feeling the pressure. I still have to manage how I'm going be in good relations with my family back home. Support them, as well as supporting my family and myself. So, it's kind of like three different bridges that I'm crossing at the same time: myself, my family, and my major. … I still talk to [my family] and I don't really ignore them, I listen to them, but I am the one who makes the decisions at the last.—Hamza

> I sort of resonate with you when you said I have a different identity when I am at work, when I'm at school, when I'm with my friends. I'm queer, so like at work I'm definitely not queer; at school I'm rarely queer; but in my personal life, I am queer as the day is long. I am also multi-ethnic, and it is strange being part of so many different families, having so many different things making me who I am. I'm trying to figure out well, who am I today? Who am I in this environment? And like, how do I identity with myself and my sister, my friends, and that sort of thing, it's kind of hard.—Sierra

Burden of Privilege

The Burden of Privilege theme examines how FG students define their independence, with a constant eye to their obligations and responsibilities back home, in an effort to reap the benefits of a college education. This theme reflects a realization of what is both gained and lost in coming to college. In Different Worlds, students express frustration about the disparate and incompatible expectations of their worlds and efforts to become facile in border crossing. Many move beyond this, cultivating a space of interdependence—where they realize their deep responsibility to their family but also begin to assert their own direction with regard to career and life choices. These students experienced a sense of freedom, fulfillment, independence, and pride in their matriculation to college coupled with awareness that this was not a solo journey of individual choice.

They valued the space college had given them to cultivate and discover new passions and dimensions of self-hood while attending to the reality that this privilege carried with it obligations to family and community. Students were constantly carrying out a cost-benefit analysis when it came to their decisions and actions in college. These costs included the obvious financial investment in their education but also how their choices would impact the future of their families and communities. As such, their sense of independence was uniquely situated in finding interests and passions in college while also attending to how these interests could be translated into career paths that would support the upward mobility of their families. The opportunity to attend college also placed them in a privileged group. While facing seemingly insurmountable challenges, students also saw the chance to pursue a degree as a privilege—"cursed and blessed" at the same time (Pérez, Cortés, Ramos, & Coronado, 2010, p. 35). This was a position many were not accustomed to, as Olga, a multiracial student, expressed:

> Just being at the University, we are all in a place of privilege, and just realizing that, like does it matter? It does matter how we got here and the process, we have to respect that but just [also] understanding that we are in a place of privilege compare[d] to everyone else in the world.

Many students felt they had been chosen to represent their families and communities, which are illustrative of the gratitude and pressure participants felt for the opportunity to pursue their bachelor's degrees. This was an honor that would not only change their lives, but the lives of their parents, siblings, and future generations. Kaja, an African American student, captures how she viewed this opportunity:

> I wouldn't say I am the most spiritual person in the world … but to have that experience and, like, just to know that God looked out for me. I could have been anywhere in this world, you know what I'm saying, and just had kids, or have sort of mental illness, and still be living at home. But I am not there, I am here getting an education … making a way for my mother and my cousins, and my children, you know what I'm saying?

Several participants believed in a higher power and felt they were meant to navigate this path, not just for themselves but their families. This notion of a higher power was sometimes expressed in terms of religiosity, either through a particular faith or a reflection of a cultural frame of spirituality wherein students' attributed the role of destiny or fate to their position as college students (Astin, Astin, & Lindholm, 2011; Nash & Murray, 2010). Spirituality and this notion of destiny also served as a coping mechanism for participants, especially when they experienced adversity. Laticia, an African American student, speaks to this belief in destiny and the role of faith as a driving force in sustaining her through college:

> With my experience, [the] only thing that comes to mind is predestined, that's how I have to explain it. Because otherwise I can't tell you why it is as it is. I'm another very spiritual person, and I feel like that's the only way I got through. There [were] some times where … I have reached out and you still don't get [support] and so now I am extra lonely because I have already tried the people around me to get through. So just [using] prayer and realizing this is obviously meant to be and everything I am going through was going to make me stronger … I just felt like it was all supposed to happen the way it is, I am here because I'm supposed to be.

Students' comments reflect how religious, spiritual, and cultural belief systems inform and interact with choices in their microsystems of school and career planning. Although participants were grateful to be able to pursue their bachelor's degrees, they realized this privilege came at a price; they had to prove that they were worthy of this opportunity to themselves, their families, and doubters who did not believe in them. In addition, they needed to attend to the financial security of their family, serve as role models in their communities, and balance these demands with their own individual goals and interests. Students also wanted to repay their parents for the sacrifices they made to send them to school, especially since many parents worked low-paying, manual labor jobs. Participants felt responsible for their family's financial future and hoped the higher earning potential that was possible with a college education would provide their families with a better life. Mariah, an Asian American, reflected on her parents' sacrifices, while Kevin, a White student, talked about the responsibility to gain the most out of college and give back to his family:

> My parents worked their whole life, and it's really, you know, tedious jobs, it's a lot of labor work. So they are saying, if you get money through your education, it's much better than having some job, and getting paid minimal wage cause that's what they don't want me to do. Therefore, they push me to do better, and I mean it's a good thing, but at the same time, it can be a lot of pressure.—Mariah

> The stress of … wanting to graduate as soon as possible, so you can help [your] family … Because my dad's retired, you know, my family doesn't have a lot of money. So, the sooner I get a job, the better I can help my family out.—Kevin

Having had little guidance regarding getting to and through college, many FG and/or immigrant students felt compelled to serve as role models and "lay a framework" for the success of siblings and cousins. Kevin's comment describes the push-pull between learning to navigate the college process while also being expected to lead:

> You're experiencing this for yourself, and then, you know, you're paving the way for, hopefully, other brothers and sisters going [to college] and having them be able to rely on you. So, not having that reliability, or that comfort of talking to someone about it, you know it's kind of a little stress.

Although the role model position produced some stress, it also was a positive force for many of the students in this study. Participants knew their journey would not only make a difference in their lives, but for others, too, as Shannon, an African American student, noted:

> Well as far as setting an example, I'm the oldest … So, everything that I'm doing is, so that [my two younger sisters] can see something that will motivate them to want to do more. And as far as worth it, I mean we've talked about overcoming and facing adversity and feeling alone and going through these hard times, and I'm sure every single one of us would, in the end, say that this is all worth it, because this is going to get us somewhere higher … So even though it's harder for us as first-generation, in the end, we all know that being here has benefited us more than not being here would.

As participants grappled with the expectations of their families, they realized their parents only wanted what was best for them, and since parents were not college educated, they had to take their expectations with a grain of salt. Students wanted to make their parents proud but realized family advice and expectations were not always appropriate or realistic. Thus, participants started to walk the delicate line of cultivating their own interests, independent from their parental unit, while remaining cognizant and respectful of the family wishes. Kevin, a White student, shared how he navigated his independence from his family, while remaining connected:

> You just still want to be independent out there, you know, it's your college career—you want to experience that, but you also got to realize that you can't disappoint your family 'cause they rely on you to do well. So you can be independent to a point, but you also need to realize that [your family depends on you to be] that reliable one in your family to do well.

Awareness of the privilege of being the first in their family to attend college also heightened the students' fear of failure. Mohamed, a Somali immigrant, stated this involved "a lot of thinking to overcome the fear." This fear of failing one's family, as well as settling for choices that might make parents personally unhappy, was a source of tremendous pressure. Students acknowledged there were ways of learning to be independent while remaining connected to their roots. Hamza, another Somali immigrant, described the privilege and burden of his experience, while Justin, an African American, noted this progression would result in some missteps, but there was much to be learned from his failures:

> It's this process of psyching myself, no matter what you have accomplished you're still coming back [home].—Hamza

> I have to take responsibility for myself, so it's [going] to get a lot better. And even though I have failed a lot of times, but at the same time I need to go through that, so I can learn from my mistakes. The process is pretty good so far, I am not exactly where I want to be, but I am making pretty good progress.—Justin

Summary

Across both themes of Perpetual Border Crosser and Burden of Privilege, students addressed how they sought to negotiate the discomfort they experienced at home and at school. They commented on how they needed to re-define the idea of independence to create space for their families' hopes and dreams and their own. Both themes represent FG students' self- described developmental progression toward navigating the struggle of multiples worlds and identities. Their commentary in these themes reflects the dynamic interactions between student and environment in the ecological model as well as the extent to which students articulated increasing awareness of how internal self-perception and external contexts impacted their meaning making (Bronfenbrenner & Morris, 2006).

Finding Footholds: Establishing Voice and Call for Genuine Commitment

The final two themes in this study—Establishing Voice and Call for Genuine Commitment—examine the types of resources FG students deemed particularly helpful in their collegiate success and critique the ways in which the University failed to meet their needs. The Establishing Voice theme speaks to how individual and programmatic supports created a sense of agency and empowerment for the participants as they balanced demands of school, home, and community with individual goals and dreams. While not all students in this study became completely facile negotiating their multiple identities and contexts, their reflections regarding networking, help seeking, and giving back to their communities suggest that, with the right support, many students became more adept at meaning making and increased their sense of comfort with the hybridity of their identities.

The last theme, Call to Genuine Commitment, addresses how students' sense of agency allowed for an increasingly sophisticated understanding of institutional systems and includes some thoughtful critiques of how those systems can more effectively support low-income, FG students. These critiques reflect student perceptions of policies and funding allocations, advising, faculty mentoring, and pedagogy as components of institutional commitment to them. Their commentary suggests an increasingly complex way of understanding the intersections between their multiple contexts. For example, students were able to see how financial aid and institutional policies (exosystem) interacted with employment and home and school worlds (microsystems). It should be noted, however, that the participants in this study reflect FG students who had been retained and cannot, therefore, speak for those students who had left the institution.

Establishing Voice

This theme addresses how students began to take control of their experiences by networking, finding safe spaces, engaging in leadership opportunities and community engagement. It captures the students' growing sense of empowerment while negotiating the processes of border crossing and managing their burden of their privilege.

Establishing Voice captured how students relied on and benefited from key programmatic supports and individual mentorship from staff, faculty, and peers to build a foundation that gave them confidence, the ability to thrive, and a sense of belonging in campus settings. In the process of finding their own voice on campus, many students reported a need to make a difference in the lives of others. In particular, the feeling of reciprocity was directed back to their communities and to the youth they hoped would follow in their footsteps. The Burden of Privilege theme represented the sense of obligation that accompanied matriculation to college. In Establishing Voice, students referred to volunteer opportunities, internships, and nonprofit organizations, both on and off campus, where they found their social capital validated, often by staff and young people whose life experiences mirrored their own.

In all of the focus groups, participants acknowledged programs that helped them get acquainted with college life. These included the Summer Bridge program; TRIO Student Support Services; McNair Scholars; specific multicultural advising offices on campus; University-wide multicultural programs that allowed space and leadership opportunities for a critical mass of low-income, FG students of color; and scholarship programs providing financial support, tutoring, leadership, and engagement opportunities. These initiatives shared some common features in design and practice, such as fostering opportunities to create a peer network, bridging the academic and social worlds of FG students, integrating academic and social engagement options, and creating a safe place to cultivate relationships with adult advisors who assisted the students for the duration of their college careers.

The most cited initiative was the Summer Bridge program that provided low-income, FG students with on-campus housing and enrollment in one to two credit-bearing course(s) with a cohort of peers. When effectively designed, such programs can serve to create a sense of ownership and belonging for students who may otherwise feel like they are on the fringes of campus life. Part of this acculturation process includes time to explore campus resources and connect with mentors and peers, as well as consider the unwritten rules and expectations of academia (i.e., informal and informal structures of higher education). Moreover, participants in this program received social support from advisors and formed lasting friendships that translated to a peer safety net.

These supports helped students establish voice by providing a safe space for participants to begin exploring academic life and integrating them socially into campus life. In the Bridge program, for example, students established lasting friendships and remained connected with this group throughout college. They were able to reach out to this group of peers in times of stress and felt they had trusted friends. These peers understood the participants' challenges because they had similar lived experiences. Students also credited this program with helping them find a sense of belonging on campus. Participants knew they had a safety net in Bridge support, and, because of this, they were more confident about exploring the college experience. May Lor, a Hmong immigrant student, talked about what being part of the Bridge program meant to her:

> So, there were times when it was pretty scary, but then, after going through it [Bridge], I always know that I have people I can rely on, I have people I can network with … and, I had great mentors, too, that helped me along the way. And, so, it wasn't really that scary after all.

Chris, a Native American student, added that the advantage of such programs is that students not only retained cohort connections throughout their collegiate careers but also returned to the program as peer leaders:

> I think it helped both being a participant and being a counselor because, like, I got introduced to things that I didn't know what to expect up here. Bridge kind of structured that … showed me how hard I had to work. I had to step up my game. [Bridge] prepared me that way and prepared me to be away from my family.

TRIO programs and multicultural centers were viewed favorably by students because they offered advising, tutoring, access to resources, and provided a space for students with similarly intersecting demographic characteristics (e.g., race, class, immigrant status) to gather. These programs often became locations where students felt their multiple identities were validated and reinforced. In addition, because many of these initiatives had common gathering spaces and leadership opportunities, they served as a loosely structured peer support system. Many of the participants formed relationships, both formal and informal, that made their college experience more meaningful. TRIO also afforded students the opportunity to be surrounded by staff members who were invested in them (i.e., institutional agents), which served as a motivating factor. Tina, a Thai immigrant, talked about the support she received from being part of TRIO:

> To have that kind of support from people [TRIO] who do know and who do care about your
> success. … that's very important and also something that motivates me. Now there are people
> who are holding me accountable. I feel like I have to be successful because there are people help-
> ing me. You know, they're invested in this as well. So like skipping classes and stuff, "no that doesn't
> work out" because I know people in my classes, they know me, and we're going to look out for
> each other.

Students also valued advising professionals giving them access to designated meeting spaces and resources, such as study rooms, computers, and printing services. Other on-campus services, including student cultural organizations, multicultural student support services, and advising and tutoring services, were useful; however, there were limitations as to the extent to which these were cited as consistently supportive.

Scholarships and related programming were important to student success because they provided financial resources with embedded advising and support for recipients. Representatives from these scholarship programs were often located on campus, so participants had access to additional staff when needed. Many of these scholarship programs were specifically available to students who were met FG and/or low-income criteria and often included students who were historically underrepresented in the academy. Applications required demonstration of academic merit, and monetary awards were frequently attached to maintaining good academic standing and volunteering in the community. Participants' knew these scholarship programs were invested in them, and they were motivated to succeed to prove that they deserved the funds supporting their educations. In these programs, the students had personal relationships with their scholarship advisors and peers and were able to reach out to these mentors in times of stress. Monica, an African American student, talked about the difference her scholarship program made:

> It [scholarship] was helpful because it really took the financial burden off of my shoulders. After
> the money is taken off the table, I was able to focus on school pretty much over the years. The
> [scholarship] program initially set us up with a mentor and our advisor … we became close as a
> group [other scholars], so we talked to each other for [support] on different things.

As students progressed in college, the TRIO McNair Scholar's program helped them achieve another level of agency. In this program, college juniors and seniors participated in a 10-week, intensive, research apprenticeship where they were mentored by faculty members and were able to conduct research, preparing them for graduate school. These students felt empowered in this program because faculty members mentored them one-on-one. In addition to learning about the research process, they gained access to new resources that helped prepare them for graduate school experiences and expanded their personal and professional networks.

Justin, an African American student, noted that TRIO programs served as a central location where peers and staff who had lived experiences similar to the students provided "guidance through this jungle":

> Kind of like problem solving — like whether it's financial, or academic, or connecting to profes-
> sors. Something that is kind of centered around people, who have actually been through this even
> if they are administrators and staff who can share their experiences. And just coming up with ways
> to counteract [challenges] and how to deal with first-generation experiences and things like that.

Another strategy used to establish voice was networking. Many of the students combined networking and the development of leadership skills. Networking was the most important strategy for many of the participants' future success because it opened doors that resulted in access to resources. As Ali, a Somali immigrant student, stated, "It's more about who you know, more than what you know … you can come into good hands sometimes."

Networking through these programs allowed students to access resources and receive support that would not have been possible without these contacts. To complement what Ali said, Sabra, another Somali immigrant student, added, "Yeah, it's who you know, but at the same time it's really about who knows you."

The value of knowing and being known was reflected in mentoring relationship that included both peers and key staff. Britney, an African American, shared how advisors who used holistic advising practices were instrumental in celebrating the students' successes and supporting them through challenges and decision making:

> They [advisors at the multicultural advising center] actually really take the time to sit down and meet with you and get to know you a little bit more … on a personal level. Like, she knew what was going on with me; she was able to, like, give me her personal opinion for what would be best for me in that situation, considering my academic and personal life at the time,

The programs that supported these students in their development as scholars also offered opportunities to cultivate leadership skills and connect with other students, including older peer mentors. Many participants also chose to get involved in student groups; they wanted to have a voice on campus. Monica, an African American student, explained,

> When people are willing to help, you [listen to] their advice … I am in the Black Student Union. There [was] a senior that was graduating, I was a year behind her, but she let me know what kind of things that she did that year to get her to graduation.

Students noted that in addition to feeling understood by staff and peers in Bridge and TRIO programs, another key commonality was timing and the way in which the programs served as practice grounds for the work that lay before them. The Bridge initiative was a precursor to their first semester in college and the competitive McNair Scholars program that happened in the junior and senior years, which in turn preceded applications to graduate school. Yang, a Hmong immigrant who participated in both, reflects on the value of scaffolded preparation:

> I would say the Bridge program as well as the McNair program is kind of a prep program, it prepares you for something coming. What those programs have done. … you kind of go through the motions before the motions come … it's kind of like a mock classroom. You go through the experience and what it does it prepares you for the real deal.

Establishing genuine relationships was also important to participants' success. Emily, a White student, talked about the difference connecting with a professor made to her academic success:

> The first 25 minutes of class he [professor] spent talking about, you know, how we're all going to go to grad school, and he is going to make sure of it and that he's going to set us up for it, and he's not like other teachers, and he'd be there to write us recommendations letters, and he's there to talk to us. It was so weird 'cause he taught production, which had nothing to do with it, but he just cared about his students so much that he wanted to touch each of them and did. I mean [if he hadn't written] my letter of recommendation to McNair, I would [have] never been in here.

Participants acknowledged there were professors who were focused on teaching and mentoring as a central component of their jobs, while others were less invested in these aspects. Although students got discouraged if their attempts to reach out to professors were not successful, they also stressed there were professors who cared about their students' and wanted them to succeed in their classes and beyond. When instructors were invested in teaching and mentoring, this passion was apparent, and the students had positive experiences in the classroom and connected more easily with faculty. These instructors used pedagogical approaches that appealed to a variety of learning styles and engaged students in the content—making the students want to reciprocate. May Lor, a Hmong immigrant, talked about the difference an instructor's dedication made to her learning:

> He was more interactive, and he really engaged students in his class, and his assignments were really worthwhile … we had debates; we had multiple discussions; we would go outside and even play dodge ball. I think it was just his teaching style, and his teaching style was really different from a lot of other teachers that I had.

Other students commented on the impact of creating a classroom community where faculty facilitated meaningful interactions between students. These interactions were often project-based or discussion-oriented and provided students with the opportunity to connect with peers during class. Participants who were not yet engaged on campus valued this additional community building, as Yang, a Hmong immigrant student, confirmed:

> [In] a lot of classes that we have here we don't really get to know our peers. For me, I would say it helps when faculty connect us to our classmates. … because, I mean, as a first-generation student, I wasn't connecting to any organization here or anyone outside of the classroom, and so allowing students to connect in the classroom would branch out our experience.

Many of the study participants also found their voice by continued involvement in communities outside the University. Students realized it was a privilege for them to be attending college and wanted to use this opportunity to make a difference for others. Hamza, a Somali immigrant student, had attended a suburban high school, where minority, low-income, FG students did not receive any mentorship to consider attending college. He wanted to change that and talked about why giving back was important to him:

> Nobody thinks about any minority or first-generation students. So my goal was, I knew some individuals who are very talented … who can do better than me, but they really don't have the, you know … the thinking that they can do it. I'm pretty sure I have influenced a lot of them. Now they have full-time scholarships and go to like different schools. … So, it's kind of like that (I) set an example … I'm impacting somebody's life to be better.

Participants wanted to "pay it forward" to let other low-income, FG students to know that college was possible. This dream was achievable, as Justin, an African American student, demonstrated:

> I am a U Scholar, so during the school period, I go back and volunteer in my elementary school, and it feels great to be there because I am able to show the students there that college is possible, which is rewarding.

Although many of the participants were able to navigate the academic environment by the end of their college careers, the students noted that obstacles they faced along the way could have been avoided if they had access to strong holistic advising, peer mentoring, and financial resources at the beginning of their college careers. Throughout their educational journeys, students gained confidence and established their voices in varied ways; yet those who received early support arrived at this point sooner because they had a trusted network of peers, faculty members, and mentors. Students developed strong navigational skills, knowing how to successfully access University-wide resources. They felt a sense of belonging and privilege through their on-campus involvement with multicultural centers, TRIO, advisors, and professors, as well as their off-campus community efforts; as result, these students found their voice and persisted toward their goals.

Call to Genuine Commitment

As the title of this theme suggests, many students questioned the authenticity of the commitment that institutions have to their success. Participants were disheartened about the dwindling resources supporting the success of historically underrepresented students in academia and the broken financial promises from this institution. They were especially unnerved and visibly disappointed about the elimination of the University's Summer Bridge program that created space for both academic and social integration on campus, as well as diluting or cutting other key programs. Monica, an African American, commented on the necessity for policies and places that actively support students:

> We have had so many problems with our cultural centers being threatened. … or our money being taken away from us, so that policy—it really needs to stand behind [us] and recognize that diversity really does improve the atmosphere of the campus.

Speaking to the decreased funding across higher education and the implications this has for how campuses allocate resources, many students resonated with what James, an African American student, called "the corporatization of education." For Sabra, a Somali immigrant, this corporatization included a promotional strategy around diversity that seemed hollow:

> When I hear diversity at the University, I just think of a marketing tool—that's what it is used for, in terms of racial diversity and cultural diversity, universities have general statements of "Oh we value everyone, blah, blah, blah". … I think of it as a selling point.

Financial support and admissions were two areas that students repeatedly alluded to in their assessment of policies and procedures that impact their success. As expressed in the early themes of Visible/Invisible and Different Worlds, financial stressors were significant obstacles to the completion of a college degree for many. Students unequivocally championed programs that provided financial grants throughout their college careers and attributed the consistency of this guaranteed support as critical to their success. Seng, a Hmong immigrant, pointed to a now defunct partnership program between K-12 city schools and the University that provided financial aid for low-income students of color for the duration of four years in college. He noted that this support allowed him the time to become more engaged in campus organizations and his academic work:

> If we didn't have that scholarship, I figured I would be working … so really it is a burden off my shoulders, and it is a burden off my parents' shoulders too.

The challenge came when programs, like those noted above, began with the promise of financial support only to have the support pulled out after the first year, as administrators' foci changed or new administrators at the institutions re-allocated the funds for other projects. Sabra, noted the disappointment and frustration with these broken promises:

> When I first came to the University, they gave me a promise, it no longer exists. … There is a University expectation from us, as a general student or student of color or students who are underrepresented, or even first-generation—we are expected to excel, but I feel like the University gets less and less invested in us every single year, whether that be in scholarships or just different things [supports].

Students also commented on the relationships between shrinking financial supports for FG students and what they perceived as more stringent admissions policies that limited access to historically marginalized students. Tina, a Thai immigrant, observed,

> Step by step, the access to [college] for a first year for students of color is getting harder, and one of the things that made me come to this [institution] than go somewhere else was I was promised when I had applied … regardless of how much financial aid award you get, the [institution] will

fill the gap" and that was a promise in which I graduated in four years. I had that promise, but if that doesn't exist anymore … the ladder just gets higher and higher for the next generation of first-gen students. So, it's not about the ones that are already here, it's the ones who aren't going to have access.

The essential need for effective institutional agents and on-campus advocates as mentors and guides was another concern raised by students. While many touted the strong and meaningful advising relationships they developed with staff in TRIO programs and multicultural offices, students expressed frustration with academic advising outside these locations. Their critique was not a blanket rebuke of all advisors but rather what they experienced as a lack of consistency in knowledge of subject matter, understanding of their lived experience, and availability to support them holistically.

James, an African American student, thought the role of an advisor was to "help us figure out our path;" yet, often the interaction and limited time with the advisor led to a focus on the mundane and necessary components of course registration—without the opportunity for meaningful career planning or relationship building that many FG students need. May Lor, a Hmong immigrant, speaks to this:

> I think for me it's just knowing the face … I had four different advisors throughout my undergraduate year. It was a lot of people who I have to go to through to get like holds off, to register for classes, get permission numbers, there's just a lot of those, systemic things.

Several students reported discomfort with revealing their true concerns to advisors because their collegiate life did not fit the mold of "typical" college students, and they did not feel their concerns would be seen as legitimate. Emnet, an Ethiopian immigrant, said,

> I didn't really feel that connection. Even to be able to tell them what I'm struggling with, I kind of kept myself from telling them what I'm going through because I felt like I was being judged.

Others noted the lack of relationship and context building resulted in meetings that felt more like they were being tracked for certain paths, rather than discussing their interests and goals. Emily, a White student, reported,

> There are advisors who don't care about you, they don't really look into your interest and what you're good at and try to help you chose a good career path. They just were like, "Oh well your grades aren't good enough to do biology, so you're going to have to get rid of that dream. How about psychology? You took psychology and got an A. Let's just make you a psychology major." You know … it's like that's not good.

These grievances raise important questions about institutional resources, training, and support allocated to advising staff that are often the first line of interaction with many students. Comments reflected an increased need for advising and career planning that holistically addresses FG student issues. While students spoke to critical role of navigators (i.e., advisor, peers, and faculty) propelling them forward, they were quick to note that many faculty would benefit from a better understanding of experiences of FG college students.

When reflecting on their classroom experiences—where college students spend the bulk of their scheduled time—participants had feedback for faculty in the following areas: understanding FG context, classroom climate, pedagogical approaches, and mentoring. Students called on faculty to be as Sabra, a Somali immigrant, put it,

> Understanding that we might not necessarily fit the average student at the University because of our circumstance, or the place that we are at in our lives. Some of us may have more obligations because of where we are from, and because we are first-generation. So, just [have] an open mind about that and not make assumptions.

Sierra, a multiracial student, added that this process of understanding different students in classroom requires,

> Being sensitive to the fact that we are not all the same. We do not come from the same background. We do not all come from the same advantages. We are not the same; do not treat us like cattle.

With regard to understanding the experience of FG students, participants were quick to note that they did not want pity or special treatment but rather a willingness on the part of the faculty to, as Thomas, a Native American student, said, "listen … have a little bit more empathy, [and] think about what it's like to be in our shoes." This call for better understanding the context of FG students is reflective of the Visible/Invisible, Different Worlds, and Perpetual Border Crosser themes where students expressed the impact of isolation, both at home and on campus. When faculty are attuned to the multiple identities and contexts in which FG students on their campus live, they may be less likely to perpetuate isolation or labeling in their own classrooms. They may also be more cognizant of why a student might be grappling with balancing familial responsibilities and college work. The intent is not to absolve the student of responsibility but to create interactions that reflect an understanding of their lived experience. As such, many students talked about needing help reaching out to faculty to overcome the intimidation they felt in college and particularly in large classes. Participants hoped that faculty would be more willing to facilitate an appropriate and supportive relationship with students who are new to the academy. Emnet, an Ethiopian immigrant, shared the intimidation she felt approaching faculty:

> For me, like, especially my first and second year, it was really intimidating to approach a professor at all, and I mean I, this is probably something that everybody can like relate to, but just like finding ways to ease that relationship between professors and students.

Students often reported looking for guidance or an opening from faculty members that would signal the opportunity to have a conversation. They clearly saw value in engaging meaningfully with faculty; these interactions can be validating and powerful, as Samir, an Egyptian immigrant, illustrates:

> Because it's hard, like, talking to them. It's a pressure, so if they talk to you, like, you would feel this is important. Like, I feel important, so I would go and talk to them again.

Yet, students reported that often in office hours, there was little time and attention to connecting even at the most basic level. Melat, another Eritrean immigrant, commented on the value of having faculty who model engagement with students versus those who do not:

> So, for me, when I go to their office hours, it's nice when they actually take one minute to have a good conversation like, "How are you? How's the class?" You know, "Do you have any suggestion like that." I don't really get that from a lot of my science classes, and I take so many science courses. It's, like, you go to like office hours, and [there are] three, four students in the office with you, so you don't even get that one-on-one. And it's usually like, "Do you have a problem?" it's not even, like, "oh hi, hello?" So, it's really hard, so I wish our professors [were] more friendly and caring and just give you that little attention where, like, they do care, and they want you to understand what they're teaching you, and it feels nice.

Students were also aware they were part of the relational process and needed to challenge themselves to approach faculty to cultivate meaningful supportive relationship. Britney, an African American student, offered this advice:

> I think just to inform students that professors are people too, so at the same time, there's a lot of insensitive professors, but there's a lot of professors that you can really sit down and talk to them

and let them know what's going on, and they'll be willing to work with you. Like, maybe break that intimidation factor where you can have a healthy dialogue with your professors because sometimes if you stand out to your professors, that's what helps you shine through.

Study participants encouraged faculty to be willing to humanize themselves—to share a little bit about their work and their interests beyond their discipline. Many invited faculty to facilitate a conversation about communication preferences and expectations, to create a medium for initiating student-faculty interaction. While many faculty members might be willing to support or mentor students, they may assume that all students are equipped to initiate these interactions. In reality, many FG students have little experience or coaching in how to reach out to faculty, including understanding the parameters of the student-faculty relationship.

Summary

These last two themes, Establishing Voice and Call for Genuine Commitment, demonstrate how these low-income, FG students, over time, developed a nuanced and rather sophisticated view of the institutional and systemic forces that both supported and constrained them. They also appeared more adept at negotiating the gaps between their contexts, and they moved with greater fluidity between their identities. Yet, their reflections also suggest that the journey to deeper meaning making about self and context is not easy, and, in many cases, they "chanced" into the people, places, or programmatic support that eventually sustained them toward graduation. Students expressed concern for the lack of effective coordination and intentionality of resources for future FG students. The final section will make an argument for collective ownership of FG student success across administrative, faculty, and student affairs units and provide suggestions for implementing more cohesive efforts to support FG college students as they persist toward completing their college degrees.

Discussion and Implications

When discussing persistence, student success, and the pathway to graduation for low-income, FG students, Engstrom and Tinto (2008) argued that "access without support is **not** opportunity" (p. 50). Building on this contention, this section (a) synthesizes the findings of this study, (b) outlines and describes specific recommendations and tools of practice for higher education professionals and institutions, and (c) offers suggestions and points out limitations regarding future research on FG students.

Themes

In addition to the six themes—Visible/Invisible, Different Worlds, Perpetual Border Crosser, Burden of Privilege, Establishing Voice, and Call for Genuine Commitment—drawn from the students' comments and discussed in detail in the previous sections, five underlying ideas were consistent across all of them. They were the importance of (a) context, (b) family and home community, (c) a sense of place, (d) meaningful connections, and (e) expectations.

Context and the interaction of contextual factors between the students and their environments were paramount. All the students discussed the challenges of assuming multiple roles and balancing responsibilities in diverse and complex contexts (e.g., school, home, work). From an ecological perspective, the students' microsystems (e.g., school, family, social class) and their interactions within different environments (i.e., mesosystems) were diverse and multifaceted. Moreover, the *meaning* that students assigned to these interactions was especially rich. These experiences helped inform and enrich their identities as FG students while making the transition from high school to college. Context mattered. Each student had a different story, despite some commonalities, and they wanted to be seen by others at the university (e.g., faculty members and advisors) as unique individuals, underscoring that FG students are not a homogenous group.

Numerous students commented on the vital role that **family** played in their personal and academic journeys. Students who were first in their families to go to college faced multiple challenges—including the pressure to continually balance the responsibilities of being a full-time student while simultaneously meeting expectations at home. These responsibilities often included taking care of siblings, and in many cases, providing financial support to their families. Additionally, students experienced pressure to succeed and to honor family expectations (while also attempting to claim some sense of personal independence). Students discussed the dilemma of pursuing their own interests and dreams while attending to how their academic degree would impact the future financial mobility of their families. Many students felt both "cursed and blessed" (Pérez et al., 2010, p. 35). On one hand, they face seemingly insurmountable challenges, yet they also feel grateful with a sense of privilege for having the chance to pursue a college degree. This push-and-pull tension was experienced by most of the students in the study. Though parents may not have fully understood the expectations of college—sometimes resulting in unrealistic or conflicting demands that created additional stress for students—most of the families were integral and involved in the multiple aspects of the students' experiences. Family members were key factors in the microsystem (most proximal) dimension for students. For example, family and community expectations and messages about "acceptable" career and major options clearly overlap with the salience of context from an ecological perspective.

Depending on how and when these students connected with timely supports (e.g., mentors, programs), they tended to find a **sense of place** despite their challenges as perpetual border crossers. Experiencing a feeling of belonging at this PWI was not easy for most of the participants, many of whom were students of color and/or immigrants. Unfortunately, several students experienced various forms of discrimination, and unintended slights (often based on race, ethnicity, or dress), which Sue (2010) called *micro-aggressions*. Many experienced feelings of marginalization, existing on the fringe of classroom and campus experiences (i.e., visible yet invisible). Despite these challenges, the students in this study gained confidence and successfully found ways to get involved at the university and benefitted from specific support structures across the institution. As noted in the Establishing Voice theme, students found their way by getting involved in different student organizations where they had critical mass (e.g., student clubs and identity-based organizations); making strong connections with peers; and establishing relationships by getting involved on campus. Other students in the study become even more active on campus, taking leadership roles and becoming socially and politically active. The students shared both positive and negative experiences in terms of their engagement and sense of place at this PWI. For instance, students articulated ideas about improving campus diversity initiatives and improving the quality of student interactions with faculty members and institutional agents on campus (e.g., academic advisors) to enhance perceptions of belonging on campus.

Students talked about the value of making **meaningful connections** with peers but also faculty members, advisors, and others across campus—often through programs and initiatives designed for FG and immigrant students. Participants frequently commented on the importance of transition initiatives, such as the Summer Bridge program, as a way to build valuable relationships with other students and learn the landscape of the University before the start of the fall semester. Additionally, students benefitted from multicultural student support services, scholarship opportunities, and the McNair Scholars program for undergraduate research. These initiatives not only helped establish meaningful connections and networks, especially with faculty members and advisors, but also provided a sense of home for many FG students, especially those who identified as students of color. Further, students noted that organizations that embraced their multiple identities were critical to their success, particularly those where they felt understood and did not always need to explain themselves. Also noted was the value of that critical faculty or staff member who served as a mentor, resource, and support person during the college years; study participants tended to seek out these connections. This finding suggests that consistent support was a component that facilitated retention and success for these low-income, FG students.

Finally, students acknowledged they held **expectations** that were not being fulfilled by the institution. This sentiment was described in the final theme, Call to Genuine Commitment. Students called for improved institutional support. Many had concerns about funding and program initiatives that were recently discontinued (e.g., the Summer Bridge program). Funding and financial decisions often occur at the exosystem and macrosystem levels in the ecological model. Students have less control over these more distal influences, yet decisions regarding financial issues inevitably impact their experiences. As FG and immigrant students, they often expressed anxiety and concern about money, the rising cost of tuition, and the amount of time they had to work outside of school. Students felt that the academic institution should provide more financial aid opportunities to ameliorate the rising costs of attending college.

Several participants expressed disappointment and concern about the lack of diversity on campus—despite deliberate marketing efforts that depicted a demographically diverse student body. Coming from diverse high school experiences, some students anticipated and expected similar learning environments and also sought mentors who reflected their communities of origin. Instead, they experienced being the token student of color or the only immigrant in the classroom. As a result, the students often felt marginalized, isolated, and alone. Additionally, students expected more authentic engagement from faculty members and advisors. While students were often intimidated by faculty, they still sought to have stronger relationships with their instructors. Similarly, students had concerns about academic advising; notably, the structure of the advising model (e.g., high student caseloads and limited available time) prevented opportunities for genuine partnerships that allowed for holistic advising.

Recommendations for Higher Education Professionals and Institutions

Based on the study findings, this section highlights recommendations for higher education professionals and institutions that address issues identified in the six themes and ways to better serve low-income, FG, and/ or immigrant student populations. While many of these suggestions deal with several themes, they have been grouped by the themes for which we felt they offered the most salient remedy. Spanning all six themes is the need for higher education professionals to consider the scholarly literature and recommendations on the ecology of campus environments. As the study data and Bronfenbrenner's developmental ecology model illustrate, the interactions between the students and their environments significantly shaped their experiences. The seminal work by Banning (1978), as well as research on campus ecology as it relates to student development, is worth further examination—especially as it ties to the developmental ecology framework for this study (Strange & Banning, 2000).

Visible/Invisible and Divided Worlds

Create physical spaces and opportunities that foster belonging and sense of place for FG students. The students in the study talked extensively about places on campus where they felt comfortable. These spaces included multicultural centers; identity-based student cultural centers; and other student organizations linked to certain affinities. Perhaps not surprisingly, the centers and services students used on campus were important dimensions of their micro- and mesosystems and impacted them directly. It is known that a meaningful sense of belonging affects student persistence; satisfaction; and ultimately, graduation rates (Strayhorn, 2012). Further, authentic connections with peers, faculty members, and other institutional agents have the potential to empower students and are effective mediators for feelings of invisibility (Stanton-Salazar, 1997, 2011).

Physical spaces on campus can also include commuter lounges where students have a locker space to store items throughout the day and a place to socialize. Since many FG students do not live on campus primarily due to cost, family, and work obligations (Erisman & Looney, 2007), this strategy can help decrease feelings of isolation and marginalization. Moreover, student organizations focused around race, ethnicity, or multicultural student populations (e.g., La Raza, Black Student Union, Oromo Club) can foster a sense of belonging as well offer a space to share experiences as border crossers and discuss feelings of responsibility toward home and community. Additionally, some universities and colleges develop specific services (e.g., academic advising units, workshops) for immigrant students and/or English language learners— and these initiatives and services can foster a sense of belonging for FG students from these backgrounds. Such places have the potential to create communities of belonging (Parks, 2011; Strange, 2001).

Explore the impact of campus climate issues on FG students, including immigrants and students of color. Many students in the study experienced feelings of marginalization and discrimination. These incidences often took the form of micro-aggressions based on race, ethnicity, and physical appearances. Higher education professionals may opt to engage in campus climate assessments or "checks" to learn more about students' perceptions as it relates to issues of belonging on campus. Several students in the study challenged administrators and leaders to promote diversity initiatives beyond superficial levels, such as using students of color in promotional admissions materials. Further, it is important to have places where FG students have a critical mass as well as opportunities to integrate into campus life. Given the heterogeneity of FG students, programs and curriculum (e.g., first-year programs, seminars) that give students space to reflect on their multiple identities and see connections with peers from different racial and ethnic communities can be empowering.

Seek family engagement early in the college planning process and maintain it throughout the collegiate experience. Almost all the participants discussed their family members in one way or the other. Family expectations and support (microsystem factors) impacted their undergraduate experience. Retention efforts led by institutions should incorporate family members whenever feasible—and not just at orientation and graduation. Investment should begin early in the process, as early as junior high school. Oseguera, Locks, and Vega (2009) and Pérez et al. (2010) detailed several effective retention and support programs that can meet the needs of Latino/a students, including TRIO and SSS; summer bridge options; and specific programs such as Puente in California, MESA (Mathematics, Engineering, and Science Achievement) active in multiple states, the Hispanic mother-daughter program (HMDP) at Arizona State University, and Advancement Via Individual Determination (AVID), among others. Another example is UCLA's multi-ethnic Academic Advancement Program (AAP), the nation's largest university-based student diversity program (UCLA, n.d.).

Ideally, family members, community supporters, and faculty should be invited to participate in these collaborative efforts. Pérez et al. (2010) also described the value of family and campus support programs and network systems for FG immigrant students. For instance, some institutions require students and their parents to attend orientation and information sessions leading up to matriculation, often offering numerous sessions to accommodate busy schedules of working parents. Also, designing and implementing initiatives to celebrate the intermittent successes and milestones of FG students is an important objective, and these celebrations should involve family members whenever possible.

Create opportunities to build relationships and partnerships beyond the immediate university community. Several students in the study talked about managing their busy and complex lives outside school. Some students lived at home while others shared experiences of responsibilities and commitments to extended family and community members (divided worlds). As such, these students struggled to find meaningful opportunities for engagement. Higher education professionals can explore ways to partner with on-campus and off-campus constituents to engage students within their home communities and within the larger institutional community. For instance, advisors might support immigrant students to create and cofacilitate student groups and activities that link the institution and surrounding community. At the University of Minnesota-Twin Cities, the Somali Student Association sponsored an event in Minneapolis to celebrate the 50th anniversary of Somali independence. This collaborative effort helped to foster a partnership between the University and the Somali community in Minneapolis (one of the largest Somali populations outside of East Africa). These student groups may be focus on race or ethnicity or based on multicultural student populations; the impact of these groups can be especially strong at PWIs (Museus, 2008).

Another example of community partnership is a program located at CUNY (City University of New York). The initiative, CUNY Citizenship Now! is the first and only university-based organization of its kind to engage volunteers in large-scale, community-based initiatives. They reach out and provide citizenship assistance to a wide population of immigrants. Staffed by volunteers, including attorneys and paralegals, it is a valued program congruent with the institutional mission (CUNY, n.d.). These types of collaborative programs can promote engagement and connection for FG and immigrant students and involve interactions across different contexts.

Perpetual Border Crosser and Burden of Privilege

Establish peer mentoring programs and related strategies involving mentors who have managed similar experiences. Higher education professionals know that peer influence is powerful. Study participants mentioned the benefits of institutional efforts, such as programs that encouraged mentoring, networking, and social and academic engagement. Students sought out more of these opportunities and were frustrated when certain programs that created peer cohorts (e.g., Summer Bridge) were cut for what were perceived to be fiscal reasons. A key strategy in implementing mentoring programs for this population is the pairing of upper-division, FG, immigrant peers with first-year students (Dennis, Phinney, & Chuateco, 2005). For example, the President Emerging Scholars Program at the University of Minnesota matches first-year students with peer mentors to establish and work toward and reflect on at least three goals in three separate areas (i.e., personal, academic, and career) of development (University of Minnesota, n.d. – b).

Continue to develop, implement, fund, and promote successful programs that engage and support FG college students. Many students in this study felt marginalized, either due to being a student of color at a PWI or other factors (e.g., identity, social class, immigrant status). Strategic initiatives allowed them the opportunity to share their experiences as border crossers and discuss privilege. Numerous students talked about the value of being involved in the TRIO program, McNair Scholars, and multicultural student support services; yet these programs must continually fight for their existence despite their proven track records in helping engage and retain historically marginalized student populations (Palmer, Wood, Dancy, & Strayhorn, 2014). Educators at all levels of the institution can help promote these services and encourage students to use them. Further, since TRIO grants are capped to serve a limited number of students on campus, there are often many FG students who must seek support elsewhere. Drawing on the expertise of TRIO personnel to collaborate with or train staff in other campus programs would be a low-cost use of existing expertise

Also, since FG college students often rely heavily on their extended family, community, and peers for academic advice and major planning rather than seeking out institutional agents (Kim, 2009; Torres, Reiser, LePeau, Davis, & Ruder, 2006), advisors and educators may need to go where students are physically located and connect with them in peer-oriented, group formats (e.g., student organizations). Other initiatives that can be developed or expanded to include a specific FG focus include first-year experience programming (e.g., Welcome Week, orientation, common read) and support groups, career and life planning classes or workshops, and living-learning communities. Above all, there needs to be a more coordinated, campuswide approach to meeting FG student needs, especially in light of the number of students in this study who mentioned how happenstance played a role in their accessing key support programs or mentors, without which they may not have been retained.

In addition to creating new programming, there needs to be an ongoing commitment to funding it, as well as other multicultural student resources (e.g., advising, tutoring, mentoring). Higher education administrators need to commit to funding those programs that have demonstrated ongoing success through extensive assessment and evaluation measures. Often, there is money for first-year initiatives, but funding typically drops off in subsequent years. As a result, students can face challenges in the sophomore or junior year with limited support, which can prevent them from graduating in a timely manner, if at all. Increasingly, institutions have been paying attention to the so-called sophomore slump, which is especially salient to students from historically marginalized groups (Hunter et al., 2009; Schreiner & Pattengale, 2000). Services in the form of workshops and curriculum can include the spiritual needs and career development planning issues that several students discussed during the focus groups.

Infuse a FG emphasis with targeted support structures and high-impact educational practices into the curriculum. A targeted curriculum has the potential to help students feel empowered and create a sense of belonging, which can improve retention rates and enhance diversity on campus. For example, at the University of Minnesota, the TRIO Student Support Services Program has designed a one-credit, eight-week course for all incoming FG students in their programs. Rather than simply focusing on campus resources and navigation, this course explores context, identity, and personal strengths with students during their first-semester in college. The curriculum includes an examination of poverty and its impact on educational outcomes as well as the dissonance that students experience between their home and school worlds and identities. Students gain success navigating and balancing different cultural expectations—skills that can be translated into the college milieu. Providing students with a forum to discuss these challenges and strengths early on in their careers—and then giving them tools to respond—has been powerful. Preliminary course evaluations demonstrate that students feel empowered about their identity as FG students, rather than apologetic about it. Students in the program also leave with a cohort group of peer support and deep relationships cultivated with advisors who teach the class. Augsburg College has a similar initiative—East African Student to Teacher (EAST)—that focuses on recruiting, retaining, and supporting participants of East African descent to become licensed K-12 teachers (Augsburg College, n.d.).

Student engagement is critical to success for all students, including FG and immigrant students. Kuh (2008) has suggested high-impact educational practices (HIPs), such as common intellectual experiences, first-year seminars and experiences, learning communities, writing-intensive courses, collaborative projects and assignments, undergraduate research study, diversity or global-learning opportunities, and capstone courses and projects, are especially effective for underserved and underrepresented students. FG students tend to benefit significantly from involvement in HIPs (Jehangir, 2010a; Kuh, 2008). Unfortunately, students of color and FG students participate less frequently in these types of experiences than White students, but when they do, their success is greater (i.e., when compared to White students, there tends to be a compensatory effect; Kuh, 2008). Higher education professionals can create and promote these initiatives (for all students) and encourage FG students to actively participate in practices that support academic and social engagement. HIPs can also be designed to link with the American Association of College and Universities (AAC&U) Signature Work initiative, which prepares "students to integrate and apply their learning to a significant project completed across a semester of study or longer" (AAC&U, n.d., para.1). AAC&U has partnered with campuses across the county to assess the impact and value of signature work in meeting learning outcomes for all students.

While some HIPs may not lend themselves to some FG students (e.g., obstacles created by undocumented status in study abroad programs, inability to afford participation in unpaid internships), others can be integrated relatively seamlessly into existing pedagogy or programs. For example, many campuses feature a common intellectual experience for all first-year students (e.g., a common book). There are numerous books, and movies, that have a FG and/or immigrant focus that can be used to heighten students' understanding of diversity, while validating (i.e., making visible) the life experiences (i.e., different worlds and border crossers) of FG students. These include Rodriquez's (1982) autobiography, *Hunger of Memory*; Rendón's (1996) "Life on the Border"; Nazario's (2007) *Enrique's Journey*; as well as the films *Breaking Away* (Yates, 1979) and *First Generation* (Fenderson & Fenderson, 2011). Further, diversity, including the life experience of FG students, should be covered as a topic or unit in all first-year seminars and first-year experiences. These engagement strategies may provide validation to students and support them in their transition to the university during the first semester while also serving to broaden how all students consider the experiences and narratives of their college peers (Rendón, 1994).

Other HIPs that participants in this study mentioned as being beneficial were undergraduate research opportunities through the McNair Scholarship program and service-oriented projects within their communities. Both of these types of HIPs could be expanded by faculty engaging more students in various aspects of their research projects—formally and informally—and channeling community service into credit-bearing service-learning opportunities.

Collect data that demonstrate the intersection of FG student identities on campuses. Given that FG students are an increasingly diverse population, academic institutions could better tailor programmatic supports, recruitment, and financial aid or work-study opportunities if they had more complete information on the intersecting demographics of the FG students on their campus. Depending on geographic location and institutional type, attention to how FG status intersects with other characteristics, such as race, income, Pell Grant award, immigrant status and national origin, rural or urban experience, or veteran status, could inform programmatic and policy decisions about matriculation and persistence. For instance, this knowledge could shape how financial aid decisions, awards, and scholarships are allocated and distributed to FG students (e.g., the influence of immigrant status on access to award options) or help higher education professionals support the needs of students as they persist toward their degrees.

Explore innovative financial aid opportunities for FG students. Study participants discussed the myriad challenges of paying for a college education—a common dilemma shared by many undergraduates but heightened for low-income students. As Reed and Cochrane (2013) found, the financial burden for a four-year degree is becoming unwieldy for middle- and lower-class families. While numerous students in this study held jobs, they often were responsible not only for meeting their college expenses but also contributing to household incomes and supporting family abroad. Academic institutions need to commit to funding both merit and need-based scholarships, but offering a range of financial aid options for these students can increase retention and degree completion, especially since some families may not be in a position to assume loans due to cultural or religious beliefs. While many low-income students qualify for the Pell grant, additional targeted scholarships, even in small amounts, are critical and can be more meaningful if recipients are invited to a recognition event, or meet with a sponsoring advisor that creates some accountability to the funding source (e.g., grades, attendance at mentoring event). Special scholarships can be created via internal or external dollars. For example, partnerships with institutional development offices could offer opportunities to earmark contributions for FG students. Pérez, Ramos, Coronado, and Cortés (2007) described a California community college that used this strategy to create a program allowing faculty to donate a small percentage of their monthly salaries for scholarship funds for undocumented students. To further help FG students in times of extraordinary need, some institutions have even started emergency funds or food banks that students can access.

Establishing Voice and Call to Genuine Commitment

Offer professional development to educate faculty and staff on best practices to support FG students, and develop appropriate expectations and interactions. Faculty and the classroom experiences are important dimensions at the microsystem and mesosystem levels, yet it is critical to explore how this is operationalized in supporting student engagement and success. Key questions to ask include the following:

- What is the role of the faculty member in supporting FG college students?

- What contributions can faculty members make and how might their efforts complement the initiatives led by student affairs practitioners?

We often assume that all students know how to interact with faculty and staff—and find ease in doing so, but this is not always the case. Based on our focus groups, FG students typically are fearful and intimidated about approaching faculty members, especially at large institutions where class sizes can be overwhelming (this can be true for non-FG students as well). Research has shown that faculty interactions and the classroom experiences (micro-and mesosystem factors) have a significant impact on college student development, including academic self-concept (Kim & Sax, 2014; Pascarella & Terenzini, 2005).

Academic leaders can draw on the expertise within their campus to create professional development opportunities for faculty and staff in different units. For example, many student affairs professionals (e.g., TRIO staff) are well prepared to lead campuswide trainings to better understand and appreciate the needs of FG students. Stebleton, Huesman, and Kuzhabekova (2010) noted, "workshops can take the form of content-based information (e.g., providing information about changing demographics ...), or be more process-oriented (e.g., diversity training; skill-based classes)" (p. 9). Opportunities could be ongoing trainings, summer teaching and learning institutes, and curricular planning groups that allow faculty and staff to develop a deeper understanding and appreciation of these diverse students. Training topics might include (a) college student development issues; (b) enhanced cultural awareness to address conscious and unconscious stereotyping and racial profiling in student interactions and accommodate different cultural norms; and (c) collaboration strategies between academic and student affairs personnel to encourage more student-faculty interaction (e.g., taking advantage of faculty office hours, getting to know instructors outside of class). In addition, pedagogical trainings led by staff from campus teaching and learning centers could emphasize active-learning techniques to more effectively engage FG students, such as group and collaborative learning; interactive components in large lectures (e.g., small-group discussions, debates, forums); student involvement in the teaching process; contemplative practices; and assignments addressing social issues, current events, and cultural diversity (Tobolowsky, 2014). Further, instruction on how to better use technology (e.g., social media) in courses can deepen learning and encourage participation from students reticent to speak in large classroom contexts (Hottel, Martinez-Aleman, & Rowan-Kenyon, 2014). These possibilities have the potential to engage all students; however, they may be especially effective with students who are reticent to speak in large classroom contexts.

An ongoing dilemma about the role of faculty members in college teaching and learning is that while all are trained experts in their discipline, many are neither trained in pedagogy nor do they have an understanding of college student development issues. Affording such trainings as part of faculty development initiatives, multicultural teaching fellow programs, and teaching mentorships would provide faculty with the resources and context they need to better serve all students, including FG students. Some institutions have acknowledged faculty time and commitment through stipend awards.

Establish meaningful connections and reduce feelings of alienation or barriers between faculty and students. The students in our study wanted to see faculty members as scholars *and* people with whom they could have a conversation outside of the disciplinary context; they sought more authentic interactions with their faculty members. Enhanced interactions can begin with learning students' names—and their correct pronunciations. Names are important to students and the acknowledgment of each student by name can be especially powerful in building a strong student-faculty rapport. Some faculty might consider adding more opportunities for both faculty and student interaction during class time. Additionally, some instructors have implemented a self-analysis project or biographical object personal narrative that provides all students the chance to write about their own background (Jehangir, 2010b). An added advantage of this project is that non-FG students learn from peers who may have very different cultural, ethnic, and class backgrounds.

Instructors can also collaborate with staff from other programs in events, such as new student orientation, first-year seminars, or faculty-student mentoring programs. Soria and Stebleton (2012) emphasized that,

> These types of informal interactions provide first-generation students an opportunity to see faculty as real people. Faculty who were also the first in their families to attend college can provide mentorship to first-generation students as well, helping them to navigate their transition to the university and serving as a source of encouragement. (p. 682)

Dedicate services and diverse student affairs educators for FG student support. Students often noted that they wanted advisors and staff who knew their concerns and needs as FG learners. Assigned admissions contact person(s) and advisors—preferably representing the diversity within the student population—can streamline support to students (e.g., hiring more advisors from varied racial, class, and immigrant backgrounds). Support needed may come in the form of placement testing; documentation status issues; developmental education, career, and major decisions; and identification of specific academic and support services for FG students (Gray, Rolph, & Melamid, 1996). Having personnel dedicated to providing FG student services can also help institutions keep abreast of changing federal and state policies that may impact this population as well as assess the effectiveness of targeted initiatives. In addition, a monitoring system to follow and support FG students can be beneficial to measure their progress over time or to observe transfer patterns (Stebleton et al., 2010).

Implications for Research

While the intent of this study is to make a valuable contribution to the ongoing inquiry around low-income, FG college students, there are still ample opportunities for continued scholarly research in this area. This research explored the experiences of 39, low-income, FG, students (many of whom were also immigrants) at a large, research university who were nearing graduation. Further, students participated in focus groups at one moment in time, offering only a snapshot of their experience. While immigrant students made up a large proportion of this sample, we do not know a great deal about their past histories (e.g., first or second generation) or immigration status. As such, findings cannot be generalized across other student populations or institutions. With that caveat, we suggest several recommendations for future inquiry.

First, future research could include longitudinal, multi-institutional approaches to exploring FG students with attention to their intersecting identities (e.g., race, class, immigrant status, sexual orientation, ability). Most studies focus on students at one point in their academic careers. By interviewing students several times over the course of their college journey, researchers would be able to gain a better understanding of identity salience and the impact as well as evolution of contextual factors over time, more effectively capturing student development.

Second, future studies could explore the FG experience at different types of institutions and conduct comparative studies. It is likely the student experience is different at a small, private, liberal arts college compared to a large, public, research university; at institutions in different geographical locations (e.g., states with and without Dream Act legislation); and for students (especially immigrants) attending Hispanic-serving institutions (HSIs) and historically Black colleges and universities (HBCUs). Similarly, the impact of the political and global climate at the time of college attendance (e.g., 9/11, economic downturns, refugee migrations) could be explored.

Third, researchers should continue to explore how self-authorship may be related to FG students and the ecology model (i.e., interactions of diverse contexts, such as campus climate and social justice issues). Some literature has considered the longitudinal impact of meaning making in multicultural learning communities on self-authorship development of these students (Jehangir, Williams, & Jeske, 2012; Jehangir, Williams, & Pete, 2011), and this could be expanded to look at cognitive and intrapersonal development.

Finally, several students in the study discussed the value and importance of spiritual development and the meaning of faith in their lives. Spirituality in higher education is an emerging area of interest among both students and scholars (Astin et al., 2011; Nash & Murray, 2010; Sullivan, 2014). It would be fruitful to explore FG student spirituality issues and how they intersect with other dimensions of identity, as well as contextual influences, and how it fits into holistic student development. Research questions might include the following:

- Where do these students locate spaces of belonging around spirituality?

- Is spirituality directly connected to personal or collective identity, or perhaps both?

- How might a strong spiritual component tie to student persistence and student success?

- How does spirituality connect to family and culture for FG and immigrant students?

These are all relevant future research questions for further study.

Conclusion: FG Students as Pioneers

As we completed this research report, we were acutely aware of larger, macrolevel questions that expand well beyond the confines of this present study:

- How does the institution (and higher education in general) perceive, frame, and situate the experience of low-income, FG students?

- How do we work to continually move away from viewing FG students as a population on the fringe, often viewed through the lens of a deficit perspective?

- How effectively are institutions considering the changing demographics of the country in relation to their admission, and retention practices?

There is recent evidence to suggest that some institutions are intentionally exploring ways to recruit and support FG students (Carlson, 2014); we applaud these efforts. These are big questions that will in turn impact commitment, funding, and resources for improving programmatic design and practice in student affairs, faculty development, and academic affairs. We do not claim to have answers to all these inquiries; we do, however, feel a responsibility to raise these questions and to give voice to the ways the students' in this study have demonstrated the intersecting nature of their multiple contexts. Attention to these intersections seems critical to the persistence and success of FG learners. As Engstrom and Tinto claimed (2008), access to the institution simply is not enough; support is vital.

Ongoing research and practice on the experiences of FG college students merits further attention, inquiry, and institutional support. Greenwald (2012) encouraged faculty, staff, and administrators to think of FG students as "pioneers, not problems" (p. A37). We fully agree with Greenwald that FG students should be viewed as assets to the institution that are valued, not marginalized.

Higher education professionals at all levels and disciplines can play unique and important roles in supporting FG students on our campuses. By intentionally reaching out to support FG students, we have the potential to make a difference where it really matters. As authors and fellow educators, we challenge student affairs practitioners, faculty, and administrators to be bold and courageous, to defy the status quo, and to enthusiastically assume new and innovative roles that foster and promote FG student engagement and success on their campuses. This vital and enduring commitment will enhance the student experience for all, but especially FG student populations, and other historically underserved and marginalized student groups.

References

ACT (2013). *The condition of college and career readiness 2013: First-generation students.* Retrieved from http://www.act.org/newsroom/data/2013/states/pdf/FirstGeneration.pdf

Adelman, C. (2007). Do we really have a college access problem? *Change, 39*(4), 48-51. doi:10.3200/CHNG.39.4.48-51

American Association of College and Universities (AAC&U). (n.d.). *Signature works.* Retrieved from http://www.aacu.org/sites/default/files/files/LEAP/LEAPChallengeSignatureWork.pdf

Anzaldúa, G. (1999). *Borderlands/La frontera: The new mestiza.* San Francisco, CA: Aunt Lute Books.

Arana, R., Castañeda-Sound, C. L., Blanchard, S., & Aguilar, T. E. (2011). Indicators of persistence for Hispanic undergraduate achievement: Toward an ecological model. *Journal of Hispanic Higher Education, 10,* 1-15. doi: 1538192711405058

Astin, A. W., Astin, H. S., & Lindholm, J. A. (2011). *Cultivating the spirit: How college can enhance students' inner lives.* San Francisco, CA: Jossey-Bass.

Aud, S., Hussar, W., Johnson, F., Kena, G., Roth, E., Manning, E., Wang, X., & Zhang, J. (2012). *The condition of education 2012* (NCES 2012-045). Washington, DC: U.S. Department of Education, National Center for Education Statistics. Retrieved from http://nces.ed.gov/pubsearch

Aud, S., Hussar, W., Kena, G., Bianco, K., Frohlich, L., Kemp, J., & Tahan, K. (2011). *The condition of education 2011 in brief* (NCES 2011-033). Washington, DC: U.S. Department of Education, National Center for Education Statistics.

Aud, S., Wilkinson-Flicker, S., Kristapovich, P., Rathbun, A., Wang, X., & Zhang, J. (2013). *The condition of education 2013* (NCES 2013-037). Washington, DC: U.S. Department of Education, National Center for Education Statistics. Retrieved from http://nces.ed.gov/pubsearch

Augsburg College. (n.d.). *East program: Program for East African future teachers.* Retrieved August 27, 2014, from http://www.augsburg.edu/education/east/

Banning, J. H. (1978). *Campus ecology: A perspective for student affairs.* Cincinnati, OH: National Association of Student Personnel Administrators.

Banning, J. H., & Kaiser, L. (1974). An ecological perspective and model for campus design. *The Personnel and Guidance Journal, 52*(6), 370-375.

Barratt, W. (2011). *Social class on campus: Theories and manifestations.* Sterling, VA: Stylus.

Baum, S., Ma, J., & Payea, K. (2010). *Education pays 2010: The benefits of higher education for individuals and society.* New York, NY: College Board.

Baumeister, R. F., & Leary, M. R. (1995). The need to belong: desire for interpersonal attachments as a fundamental human motivation. *Psychological Bulletin, 117*(3), 497-529. Retrieved from http://dx.doi.org/10.1037/0033-2909.117.3.497

Baxter Magolda, M. B. (1999). *Creating contexts for learning and self-authorship: Constructive-developmental pedagogy.* Nashville, TN: Vanderbilt University Press.

Beegle, D. M. (2000). *Interrupting generational poverty: Experiences affecting successful completion of a bachelor's degree* (Unpublished doctoral dissertation) Portland State University, Portland, OR.

Beegle, D. (2003). Overcoming the silence of generational poverty. *Invisible Literacies, 15*(1), 11-20.

Bernard, H. R. (1995). *Research methods in anthropology: Qualitative and quantitative approaches.* Walnut Creek, CA: AltaMira.

Bhabha, H. (1994). *The location of culture.* New York, NY: Routledge.

Billson, J. M., & Terry, M. B. (1982). In search of the silken purse: Factors in attrition among first-generation students. *College and University, 58,* 57-75.

Bourdieu, P. (1977). Cultural reproduction and social reproduction. In J. Karabel & A. H. Halsey (Eds.), *Power and ideology in education* (pp. 487-511). New York, NY: Oxford University Press.

Bourdieu, P. (1990). Artistic taste and cultural capital. In J. Alexander & S. Seidman (Eds.), *Culture and society: Contemporary debates* (pp. 205-215). Cambridge, MA: Cambridge University Press.

Bourdieu, P. (1994). Distinction: A social critique. In D. B. Grusky (Ed.), *Social stratification: Class, race, and gender in sociological perspective* (pp. 499-525). Boulder, CO: Westview.

Brilliant, J. J. (2000). Issues in counseling immigrant college students. *Community College Journal of Research and Practice, 24,* 577-586. doi:10.1080/10668920050139721

Bronfenbrenner, U. (1976). The experimental ecology of education. *Teachers College Record, 78*(2), 157-204.

Bronfenbrenner, U. (1977). Toward an experimental ecology of human development. *American Psychologist, 32,* 513-531. doi: 10.1037/0003-066x.32.7.513

Bronfenbrenner, U. (1993). The ecology of cognitive development: Research models and fugitive findings. In R. H. Wozniak & K. W. Fischer (Eds.), *Development in context: Acting and thinking in specific environments* (pp. 3-44). Hillsdale, NJ: Lawrence Erlbaum.

Bronfenbrenner, U. (1994). Ecological models of human development. In *International encyclopedia of education* (Vol. 3, 2nd ed.). Oxford, UK: Elsevier. Reprinted in M. Gauvain & M. Cole (Eds.), *Readings on the development of children* (1993, 2nd ed., pp. 37-43). New York, NY: Freeman.

Bronfenbrenner, U. (Ed.). (2005). *Making human beings human: Bioecological perspectives on human development.* Thousand Oaks, CA: Sage.

Bronfenbrenner, U., & Morris, P. A. (2006). The bioecological model of human development. In W. Damon & R. M. Lerner (Eds.), *Handbook of child psychology* (6th ed., pp. 793-828). Hoboken, NJ: Wiley.

Brott, P. E. (2005). A constructivist look at life roles. *The Career Development Quarterly, 54,* 138-149. doi: 10.1002/j.2161-0045.2005.tb00146.x

Brown, C. M., II, & Dancy, E, T., II. (2010). Predominantly White institutions. In K. Lomotey (Ed.), *Encyclopedia of African American education.* (pp. 524-527). Thousand Oaks, CA: Sage. doi: http://dx.doi.org/10.4135/9781412971966.n193

Bryan, E., & Simmons, L. A. (2009). Family involvement: Impacts on post-secondary educational success for first-generation Appalachian college students. *Journal of College Student Development, 50,* 391-406.

Bui, K. V. T. (2002). First-generation college students at a four-year university: Background characteristics, reasons for pursuing higher education, and first-year experiences. *College Student Journal, 36,* 3-11.

Burdman, P. (2005). The student debt dilemma: Debt aversion as a barrier to college access. *Center for Studies in Higher Education.* Retrieved from https://escholarship.org/uc/item/6sp9787j

Cabrera, A, F., Burkum, K., & La Nasa, S. (2003) *Pathways to a four-year degree: Determinants of degree completion among socioeconomically disadvantaged students.* Paper presented at the Association for the Study of Higher Education, Portland, OR.

Carlson, S. (2014, July 28). Spending shifts as colleges compete on students' comfort. *The Chronicle of Higher Education.* Retrieved from http://chronicle.com/article/Spending-Shifts-as-Colleges/147921/

Carnevale, A. P., & Rose, S. J. (2004). Socioeconomic status, race/ethnicity, and selective college admissions. In R. D. Kahlenberg (Ed.), *America's untapped resource: Low-income students in higher education* (pp. 101-156). New York, NY: The Century Foundation Press.

Carnevale, A. P., Rose, S. J., & Cheah, B. (2011). *The college payoff: Education, occupations, lifetime earnings*. Washington DC: Georgetown University Center of Education and the Workforce. Retrieved from http://hdl.handle.net/10822/559300

Cerezo, A., O'NeiI, M. E., & McWhirter, B. T. (2009). Counseling Latina/o students from an ecological perspective: Working with Peter. *Journal of College Counseling, 12*(2), 170-181.

Chang, M. (2011). Asian American and Pacific Islander millennial students at a tipping point. In F. A. Bonner, A. F. Marbley, & M. F. Howard-Hamilton (Eds.), *Diverse millennial students in college: Implications for faculty and student affairs* (pp. 55-68). Sterling, VA: Stylus.

Charmaz, K. (2006). *Constructing grounded theory: A practical guide through qualitative analysis*. Thousand Oaks, CA: Sage.

Chatman, S. (2008). *Does diversity matter in the education process? An exploration of student interactions by wealth, religion, politics, race, ethnicity and immigrant status at the University of California* (Research and Occasional Paper Series, CSHE 5.08). Berkeley, CA: University of California, Berkeley, Center for Studies in Higher Education.

Chen, X., & Carroll, C. D. (2005). *First-generation students in postsecondary education: A look at their college transcripts* (NCES 2005-171). U.S. Department of Education, National Center for Education Statistics. Washington, DC: U.S. Government Printing Office.

Choy, S. (2001). *Students whose parents did not go to college: Postsecondary access, persistence, and attainment: Findings from the Condition of Education 2001.* (NCES 2001-126). Washington, DC: U.S. Department of Education, National Center for Education Statistics.

Choy, S. P., Horn, L. J., Nunez, A., & Chen, X. (2000). Transition to college: What helps at-risk students and students whose parents did not attend college. *New Directions for Institutional Research, 107,* 45-63.

Chung, R. H. G. (2001). Gender, ethnicity, and acculturation in intergenerational conflict of Asian American college students. *Cultural Diversity and Ethnic Minority Psychology, 7,* 376-386. doi:10.1037/1099-9809.7.4.376

City University of New York (CUNY). (n.d.). *CUNY Citizenship Now.* Retrieved from http://www.cuny.edu/about/resources/citizenship/about-us.html

Clandinin, D. J., & Connelly, F. M. (2000). *Narrative inquiry: Experience and story in qualitative research*. San Francisco, CA: Jossey-Bass.

Coffman, S. (2011). A social constructionist view of issues confronting first-generation college students. *New Directions for Teaching and Learning, 127,* 81-90. doi: 10.1002/tl.459

Davis, J. (2010). *The first generation student experience: Implications for campus practice, and strategies for improving persistence and success*. Sterling, VA: Stylus.

Deenanath, V. (2014) *First-generation immigrant college students: An exploration of career aspirations and family support.* (Unpublished master's thesis) University of Minnesota-Twin Cities, Minneapolis-St. Paul, MN.

DeAngelo, L., Franke, R., Hurtado, S., Pryor, J. H., & Tran, S. (2011). *Completing college: Assessing graduation rates at four-year institutions*. Los Angeles, CA: Higher Education Research Institute, Graduation School of Education & Information Studies, University of California, Los Angeles.

Dennis, J. M., Phinney, J. S., & Chuateco, L. I. (2005). The role of motivation, parental support, and peer support in the academic success of ethnic minority first-generation college students. *Journal of College Student Development, 46,* 223-236. doi:10.1353/csd.2005.0023

Donnelly, N. D. (1994). *Changing lives of refugee Hmong women*. Seattle, WA: University of Washington Press.

Dumais, S. A., & Ward, A. (2010). Cultural capital and first-generation college success. *Poetics, 38,* 245-265. doi: 10.1016/j.poetic.2009.11.011

Dundes, L., Cho, E., & Kwak, S. (2009). The duty to succeed: Honor versus happiness in college and career choices of East Asian students in the United States. *Pastoral Care in Education, 27,* 135-156. doi: 10.1080/02643940902898960

Engle, J. (2007). Postsecondary access and success for first-generation students. *American Academic, 3,* 25-48.

Engle, J., & O'Brien, C. (2007). *Demography is not destiny: Increasing the graduation rates of low-income college students at large public universities.* Washington, DC: The Pell Institute.

Engle, J., & Tinto, V. (2008). *Moving beyond access: College for low-income, first-generation students.* Washington, DC: The Pell Institute. Retrieved from http://www.pellinstitute.org/files/COE MovingBeyondReport Final.pdf

Engstrom, C., & Tinto, V. (2008). Access without support is not opportunity. *Change, 40,* 46-50. doi: 10.3200/CHNG.40.1.46-50

Erisman, W., & Looney, S. (2007). *Opening the door to the American dream: Increasing higher education access and success for immigrants.* Washington, DC: The Institute for Higher Education Policy.

Evans, N. J., Forney, D. S., Guido, F. M., Patton, L. D., & Renn, K. A. (2010). *Student development in college: Theory, research, and practice* (2nd ed.). San Francisco, CA: Jossey-Bass.

Fenderson, A., & Fenderson, J. [Producers & Directors]. (2011). *First generation* [Motion picture]. United States: Market Street Productions. Retrieved from http://www.firstgenerationfilm.com/about.php

Flick, U. (1998). *An introduction to qualitative research.* London, UK: Sage.

Gibbons, M. M., & Borders, L. D. (2010). Prospective first-generation college students: A social-cognitive perspective. *The Career Development Quarterly, 58,* 194-208.

Gildersleeve, R. E. (2010). *Fracturing opportunity: Mexican migrant students and college-going literacy.* New York, NY: Peter Lang.

Goodson, I. F., & Gill, S. (2011). *Narrative pedagogy: Life history and learning.* New York, NY: Peter Lang.

Graham, L. (2011). Learning a new world: Reflections on being a first-generation college student and the influence of TRIO programs. *New Directions for Teaching & Learning, 127,* 33-38. doi: 10.1002/tl.455

Gray, M. J., Rolph, E., & Melamid, E. (1996). *Immigration and higher education: Institutional responses to changes demographics.* Santa Monica, CA: Center for Research on Immigration Policy.

Greenwald, R. (2012). Think of first-generation students as pioneers, not problems. *Chronicle of Higher Education, 59*(12), A37-A38.

Gudmunson, C. G., & Danes, S. M. (2011). Family financial socialization: Theory and critical review. *Journal of Family and Economic Issues, 32,* 644-667.doi: 10.1007/s10834-011-9275-y

Guido, F. M., Chávez, A. F., & Lincoln, Y. S. (2010). Underlying paradigms in student affairs research and practice. *Journal of Student Affairs Research and Practice, 47,* 1-22. doi: 10.2202/1949-6605.6017

Hartig, N., & Steigerwald, F. (2007). Understanding family roles and ethics in working with first-generation college students and their families. *The Family Journal, 15,* 159-162. doi: 10.1177/1066480706297955

Heller, D. E. (2004). *Pell Grant recipients in selective colleges and universities* (Century Foundation Brief). New York, NY: Century Foundation.

Hinchman, L. P., & Hinchman, S. K. (Eds.). (1997). *Memory, identity, community: The idea of narrative in the human sciences.* Albany, NY: SUNY Press.

Hoare, C. (2006). (Ed.) *Handbook of adult development and learning.* New York, NY: Oxford University Press.

Hodge, A. E., & Mellin, E.A., (2010) First-generation college students: The influence of family on college experience. *The Penn State McNair Journal, 17,* 120-134.

Hoffman, M., Richmond, J., Morrow, J., & Salomone, K. (2003). Investigating "sense of belonging" in first-year college students. *Journal of College Student Retention, 4*(3), 227-56.

Horn, L., & Nuñez, A. M. (2000). *Mapping the road to college: First-generation students' math track, planning strategies and context of support* (NCES Rep. No. 2000-153). Washington, DC: National Center for Educational Statistics.

Housel, T. H. (2011). *Faculty and first-generation college students: Bridging the classroom gap together.* San Francisco, CA: Jossey-Bass.

Hottel, D. L., Martinez-Aleman, A. M., & Rowan-Kenyon, H. T. (2014). Summer bridge program 2.0: Using social media to develop students' campus capital. *Change: The Magazine of Higher Learning, 46*(5), 34-38.

Howard, A., & Levine, A. (2004). Where are the poor students? A conversation about social class and college attendance. *About Campus, 9,* 19-24. doi: 10.1002/abc.101

Hunter, M. S., Tobolowsky, B. F., Gardner, J. N., Evenbeck, S. E., Pattengale, J. A., Schaller, M., & Schreiner, L. A. (2009). *Helping sophomores succeed: Understanding and improving the second year experience*. San Francisco: CA: Jossey-Bass.

Hussar, W. J., & Bailey, T. M. (2013). *Projects of educational statistics to 2021* (NCES 2103-008). Washington, DC: U.S. Department of Education National Center for Educational Statistics.

Inkelas, K. K., Daver, Z. E., Vogt, K. E., & Leonard, J. B. (2007). Living-learning programs and first-generation college students' academic and social transition to college. *Research in Higher Education, 48*, 403-434. doi: 10.1007/s11162-006-9031-6

Ishitani, T. T. (2003). A longitudinal approach to assessing attrition behavior among first-generation students: Time-varying effects of pre-college characteristics. *Research in Higher Education, 44*, 433-449. doi: 10.1023/A:1024284932709

Jehangir, R. R. (2010a). *Higher education and first-generation students: Cultivating community, voice, and place for the new majority*. New York, NY: Palgrave Macmillan.

Jehangir, R. (2010b). Stories as knowledge: Bringing the lived experience of first-generation college students into the academy. *Urban Education, 45*(4), 533-553.

Jehangir, R., Williams, R., & Jeske, J. (2012). The influence of multicultural learning communities on the intrapersonal development of first-generation college students. *Journal of College Student Development, 53*, 267-284.

Jehangir, R., Williams, R. D., & Pete, J. (2011). Multicultural learning communities: Vehicles for developing self-authorship in first-generation college students. *Journal of The First-Year Experience & Students in Transition, 23*(1), 53-73.

Jensen, B. (2004). Across the great divide: Crossing classes and clashing cultures. In M. Zweig (Ed.), *What's class got to do with it? American society in the twenty-first century* (pp. 168-83). Ithaca, NY: ILR.

Karen, D. (2002). Changes in access to higher education in the United States: 1980–1992. *Sociology of Education, 75*(3), 191-210. Retrieved from http://www.jstor.org/stable/3090265

Kelly, P. (2005). *As America becomes more diverse: The impact of state higher education inequality.* Boulder, CO: National Center for Higher Education Management Systems.

Kent, M. M. (2007). Immigration and America's Black population. *Population Bulletin, 62*, 1-17.

Kim, E. (2009). Navigating college life: The role of peer networks in first-year college adaptation experience of minority immigrant students. *Journal of The First-Year Experience & Students in Transition, 21*(2), 9-34.

Kim, E. (2014). Breaking through a myopic view of immigrant students. *About Campus, 19*(3), 29-32. doi: 10.1002/abc.21160

Kim, E., & Diaz, J. (2013). *Immigrant students and higher education* (ASHE Higher Education Report No. 38:6). San Francisco, CA: Jossey-Bass.

Kim, Y. K., & Sax, L. J. (2014). The effects of student-faculty interaction on academic self-concept: Does academic major matter? *Research in Higher Education, 55*(8), 780-809.

Krueger, R. A., & Casey, M. A. (2009). *Focus groups: A practical guide for applied research.* Thousand, Oaks, CA: Sage.

Kuh, G. D. (2008). *High-impact educational practices: What they are, who has access to them, and why they matter.* Washington, DC: Association of American Colleges and Universities.

Lamont, M. (2000). *The dignity of working men.* New York, NY: Harvard University Press.

Lareau, A. (2002). Invisible inequality: Social class and childrearing in Black families and White families. *American Sociological Review, 67*(5), 747-776. Retrieved from http://www.jstor.org/stable/3088916

Lareau, A. (2011). *Unequal childhoods: Race, class, and family life. A decade later* (2nd ed.). Berkeley, CA: University of California Press.

Lewin, K. (1936). *Principles of topological psychology.* New York, NY: McGraw-Hill.

Lincoln, Y. S., & Guba, E. G. (1985). *Naturalistic inquiry.* Beverly Hills, CA: Sage.

Longwell-Grice, R., & Longwell-Grice, H. (2007). Testing Tinto: How do retention theories work for first-generation, working-class students? *Journal of College Student Retention: Research, Theory and Practice, 9,* 407-420.

Lucas, M. S., Skokowski, C. T., & Ancis, J. R. (2000). Contextual themes in career decision making of female clients who indicate depression. *Journal of Counseling & Development, 78,* 316-325. doi: 10.1002/j.1556-6676.2000.tb01913.x

Madyun, N., Williams, S., McGee, E., & Milner, H. R. (2013). On the importance of African American faculty in higher education: Implications and recommendations. *Educational Foundations, 27*(3/4), 65-75.

Marks, A., Turner, E., & Osborne, M. (2003). "Not for the likes of me": The overlapping effect of social class and gender factors in the decision made by adults not to participate in higher education. *Journal of Further and Higher Education, 27*(4), 347-364.

McDonough, P. M. (1997). *Choosing colleges: How social class and schools structure opportunity.* Albany, NY: State University of New York Press.

Megivern, D. (2003). Not by myself alone: Upward bound with family and friends. In V. C. Adair & S. L. Dahlberg (Eds.), *Reclaiming class: Women, poverty, and the promise of higher education in America* (pp. 119-130). Philadelphia, PA: Temple University Press.

Merriam, S. B., Caffarella, R. S., & Baumgartner, L. M. (2007). *Learning in adulthood: A comprehensive guide* (3rd ed.). San Francisco, CA: Jossey-Bass.

Mortenson, T. G (2006a). Unmet financial need of undergraduate students by state, sector, status, and income levels 2003-04. *Postsecondary Education Opportunity, 163,* 1-7.

Mortenson, T. G. (2006b). National school lunch program participation by state FFY 1993 to FFY 2005. *Postsecondary Education Opportunity, 165,* 1-8.

Mumper, M. (2003). The future of college access: The declining role of public higher education in promoting equal opportunity. *The Annals of the American Academy of Political and Social Science, 585,* 97-117. Retrieved from http://www.jstor.org/stable/1049753?origin=JSTOR-pdf

Museus, S. D. (2008). The role of ethnic student organizations in fostering African American and Asian American students' cultural adjustment and membership at predominantly White institutions. *Journal of College Student Development, 49,* 568-586.

Museus, S. D. (2011). Living at the intersection of diversification, digitization, and globalization. In F. A. Bonner, A. F. Marbley, & M. F. Howard-Hamilton (Eds.), *Diverse millennial students in college: Implications for faculty and student affairs* (pp. 69-88). Sterling, VA: Stylus.

National Survey of Education Engagement (NSSE). (2012). *Promoting student learning and institutional improvement: Lessons from NSSE at 13.* Bloomington, IN: Indianan University Center for Postsecondary Research. Retrieved from http://nsse.iub.edu/NSSE_2012_Results/pdf/NSSE_2012_Annual_Results.pdf

Nash, R. J., & Murray, M. C. (2010). *Helping college students find purpose: The campus guide to meaning-making.* San Francisco, CA: Jossey-Bass.

Nazario, S. (2007). *Enrique's journey: The story of a boy's dangerous odyssey to reunite with his mother.* New York, NY: Random House.

Nuñez, A. (2011). Counterspaces and connections in college transitions: First-generation Latino students' perspectives on Chicano studies. *Journal of College Student Development, 52,* 639-655.

Nwosu, C., Batalova, J., & Auclair, G. (2014). *Frequently requested statistics on immigrants and immigration in the United States.* Retrieved from http://www.migrationpolicy.org/article/frequently-requested-statistics-immigrants-and-immigration-united-states

Oldfield, K. (2007). Humble and hopeful: Welcoming first generation poor and working class students to college. *About Campus, 11*(6), 2-12. doi: 10.1002/abc.188

Oldfield, K. (2012). Still humble and hopeful: Two more recommendations on welcoming first-generation poor and working-class students to college. *About Campus, 17*(5), 2-13. doi: 10.1002/abc.21093

Oseguera, L., Locks, A. M., & Vega, I. I. (2009). Increasing Latina/o students' baccalaureate attainment: A focus on retention. *Journal of Hispanic Higher Education, 8,* 23-53.

Palmer, R. T., Wood, J. L., Dancy, T. E., & Strayhorn, T. L. (2014). *Black male collegians: Increasing access, retention, and persistence in higher education* (ASHE Higher Education Report No. 40:3). San Francisco, CA: Jossey-Bass.

Parks, S. D. (2011). *Big questions worthy dreams* (2nd ed.). San Francisco, CA: Jossey-Bass.

Pascarella, E. T. (2004). First-generation college students: Additional evidence on college experiences and outcomes. *The Journal of Higher Education, 75,* 249-284.

Pascarella, E. T., Pierson, C. T., Wolniak, G. C., & Terenzini, P. T. (2004) First-generation college students: Additional evidence on college experiences and outcomes. *The Journal of Higher Education, 75,* 249-284.

Pascarella, E. T., & Terenzini, P. T. (2005). *How college affects students* (Vol. 2). San Francisco, CA: Jossey-Bass.

Paulsen, M. B., & St. John, E. P. (2002). Social class and college costs: Examining the financial nexus between college choice and persistence. *Journal of Higher Education, 73,* 189-236.

Peabody, M., Hutchens, N. H., Lewis, W. D., & Deffendall, M. (2011). *First-generation college students at the University of Kentucky* (Policy Analysis Center for Kentucky Education White Paper No. 1). Retrieved from http://uknowledge.uky.edu/packe/

Perna, L. W. (2005). The benefits of higher education: Sex, racial/ethnic, and socioeconomic group differences. *Review of Higher Education, 29,* 23-52.

Pérez, W., Cortés, R. D., Ramos, K., & Coronado, H. (2010). "Cursed and blessed": Examining the socioemotional and academic experiences of undocumented Latina and Latino college students. *New Directions for Student Services, 131,* 35-51. San Francisco, CA: Jossey-Bass. doi: 10.1002/ss.366

Pérez, P. A., & McDonough, P. M. (2008). Understanding Latina and Latino college choice. *Journal of Hispanic Higher Education, 7*(3), 249-265. doi: 10.1177/1538192708317620

Pérez, W., Ramos, K., Coronado, H., & Cortés, R. D. (2007). *Developing talent: Strategies for supporting high-achieving community college students.* Symposium conducted at the Fourth Annual Tomas Rivera Policy Institute Education Conference, Long Beach, CA.

Phinney, J. S., & Flores, J. (2002). "Unpackaging" acculturation aspects of acculturation as predictors of traditional sex role attitudes. *Journal of Cross-Cultural Psychology, 33,* 320-331. doi: 10.1177/0022022102033003007

Pike, G. R., & Kuh, G. D. (2005) First-and second-generation college students: A comparison of their engagement and intellectual development. *Journal of Higher Education, 76,* 276-300.

Pittman, L. D., & Richmond, A. (2007). Academic and psychological functioning in late adolescence: The importance of school belonging. *The Journal of Experimental Education, 75*(4), 270-290.

Portes, A., & Rumbaut, R. G. (2001). *Legacies: The story of the immigrant second generation.* Ewing, NJ: University of California Press.

Ramos-Sanchez, L., & Nichols, L. (2007). Self-efficacy of first-generation and non-first-generation college students: The relationships with academic performance and college adjustment. *Journal of College Counseling, 10,* 6-18.

Reed, M., & Cochrane, D. (2013). *Student debt and the class of 2012. The project on student debt* (The Institute for College Access & Success report). Retrieved from http://projectonstudentdebt.org/files/pub/classof2012.pdf

Remington, N. (2008). *African immigrants in Minnesota.* Minneapolis, MN: The Institute for Agriculture and Trade Policy. Retrieved from http://www.iatp.org/files/258_2_104335.pdf

Rendón, L. I. (1992). From the barrio to the academy: Revelations of a Mexican American "scholarship girl." *New Directions for Community Colleges, 80,* 55-64. doi: 10.1002/cc.36819928007

Rendón, L. I. (1994). Validating culturally diverse students: Toward a new model of learning and student development. *Innovative Higher Education, 19,* 33-51.

Rendón, L. I. (1996). Life on the border. *About Campus, 1*(6), 14-20.

Rendón, L. I., Jalomo, R. E., & Nora, A. (2011). Theoretical considerations in the study of minority student retention in higher education. In S. R. Harper & J. F. L. Jackson (Eds.), *Introduction to American education* (pp. 229-248). New York, NY: Routledge.

Renn, K. A. (2003). Understanding the identities of mixed-race college students through a developmental ecology lens. J*ournal of College Student Development, 44*, 383-403.

Renn, K. A., & Arnold, K. D. (2003). Reconceptualizing research on college student peer culture. *Journal of Higher Education, 74*, 261-291.

Richardson R. C., & Skinner, E. P. (1992). Helping first-generation minority students achieve degrees. In L. S. Zwerling & H. B. London (Eds.), *First generation college students: Confronting the cultural issues* (pp. 29-43). San Francisco, CA: Jossey-Bass. doi: 10.1002/cc.36819928005

Roberts, S. (2014, August 31). Influx of African immigrants shifting national and New York demographics. *New York Times.* Retrieved from http://www.nytimes.com/

Rodriquez, R. (1982*). Hunger of memory: The education of Richard Rodriquez: An autobiography.* New York, NY: Bantam Books.

Rothkopf, A. J. (2009). Courageous conversations: Achieving the dream and the importance of student success. *Change: The Magazine of Higher Learning, 41*(1), 24-41. doi:10.3200/CHNG.41.1.24-41

Schreiner, L. A., & Pattengale, J. (2000). *Visible solutions for invisible students: Helping sophomores succeed.* (Monograph No. 31). Columbia, SC: University of South Carolina, National Resource Center for The First Year Experience and Students in Transition.

Soria, K., M., & Stebleton, M. J. (2012). First-generation students' academic engagement and retention at a large, public research university. *Teaching in Higher Education, 17*, 673-685. doi.org/10.1080/13562517.20 12.666735

Soria, K. M., Stebleton, M. J., & Huesman, R. L. (2013). Class counts: Exploring differences in academic and social integration between working-class and middle/upper-class students at large, public research universities. *Journal of College Student Retention: Research, Theory and Practice, 15(2)*, 215-242.

Staklis, S., & Horn, L. (2012). *New American in postsecondary education: A profile of immigrants and second-generation American undergraduates.* (NCES Report No. 2012-213). Washington, DC: National Center for Education Statistics.

Stanton-Salazar, R. D. (1997). A social capital framework for understanding the socialization of racial minority children and youths. *Harvard Educational Review, 67*, 1-41.

Stanton-Salazar, R. D. (2011). A social capital framework for the study of institutional agents and their role in the empowerment of low-status students and youth. *Youth & Society, 43*(3), 1066-1109.

Stebleton, M. J. (2011). Understanding immigrant college students: Applying a developmental ecology framework to the practice of academic advising. *NACADA Journal, 31*, 42-55. doi: http://dx.doi. org/10.12930/0271-9517-31.1.42

Stebleton, M. J., Huesman, R. L., Jr., & Kuzhabekova, A. (2010). *Do I belong here? Exploring immigrant college student responses on the SERU survey sense of belonging/satisfaction factor.* (CSHE Research and Occasional Paper Series 13.10). Berkeley, CA: University of California-Berkeley, Center for Studies in Higher Education.

Stebleton, M. J., & Soria, K. M. (2012). Breaking down barriers: Academic obstacles of first-generation students at research universities. *The Learning Assistance Review, 17*, 7-19.

Stebleton, M. J., & Soria, K. M. (2013). Immigrant college students' academic obstacles. *The Learning Assistance Review, 18*, 17-24.

Stephens, N. M., Fryberg, S. A., Markus, H. R., Johnson, C. S., & Covarrubias, R. (2012). Unseen disadvantage: How American universities' focus on independence undermines the academic performance of first-generation college students. *Journal of Personality and Social Psychology, 102*(6), 1178-1197.

Strange, C. C. (2001). Spiritual dimensions of graduate preparation in student affairs. In M. A. Jablonski (Ed.), *The implications of student spirituality for student affairs practice* (New Directions for Student Services, 95, pp. 57-67). San Fransisco, CA: Jossey-Bass.

Strange, C. C., & Banning, J. H. (2000). *Educating by design: Creating campus environments that work*. San Francisco, CA: Jossey-Bass.

Strayhorn, T. L. (2012). *College students' sense of belonging: A key to educational success for all students*. New York, NY: Routledge.

Stuber, J. M. (2011). Integrated, marginal, and resilient: Race, class, and the diverse experiences of White first-generation college students. *International Journal of Qualitative Studies in Education, 24*(1), 117-136.

Suárez-Orozco, C., Suárez-Orozco, M., & Todorova, I. (2008). *Learning a new land: Immigrant students in American society*. Cambridge, MA: Harvard University Press.

Sue, D. W. (2010). *Microaggressions in everyday life: Race, gender and sexual orientation*. Hoboken, NJ: Wiley.

Sullivan, W. M. (2014). Exploring vocation: Reframing undergraduate education as a quest for purpose. *Change: The Magazine of Higher Learning, 46*(4), 6-13. doi: 10.1080/00091383.2014.925753

Teranishi, R. T., Ceja, M., Antonio, A. L., Allen, W. R., & McDonough, P. M. (2004). The college choice process for Asian Pacific Americans: Ethnicity and socioeconomic class in context. *Review of Higher Education, 27*, 527-551.

Terenzini, P. T., Rendón, L. I., Upcraft, M. L., Millar, S. B., Allison, K. A., Gregg, P. L., & Jalomo, R. (1994). The transition to college: Diverse students, diverse stories. *Research in Higher Education, 35*(1), 57-73.

Tett, L. (2004). Mature working-class students in an "elite" university: Discourses of risk, choice, and exclusion. *Studies in the Education of Adults, 36*(2), 252–264.

Thomas, K. (2011). What explains the increasing trend in African emigration to the U.S.? *International Migration Review, 45*, 3-28. doi: 10.1111/j.1747-7379.2010.00837.x

Tisdell, E. J., & Swartz, A. L.(2011). *Adult education and the pursuit of wisdom* (New Directions for Adult and Continuing Education, 131). San Francisco, CA: Jossey-Bass.

Tobolowsky, B. F. (Ed.). (2014). *Paths to learning: Teaching for engagement in college*. Columbia, SC: University of South Carolina, National Resource Center for The First-Year Experience & Students in Transition.

Torres, V., Reiser, A., LePeau, L., Davis, L., & Ruder, J. (2006). A model of first-generation Latino/a college students' approach to seeking academic information. *NACADA Journal, 26*, 65-70.

Tyre, P. (2014, February 5) Improving economic diversity at the better colleges. *New York Times*. Retrieved from http://nytimes.com/

University of California, Los Angeles (UCLA). (n.d.). *Welcome to AAP*. Retrieved August 27, 2014, from http://aapucla.com/

University of Minnesota (n.d. - a). *Office of institutional research: Student financial support*. Retrieved August 27, 2014, from http://www.oir.umn.edu/student/financial_support/report

University of Minnesota (n.d. - b). *President's emerging scholars program*. Retrieved August 27, 2014, from http://prezscholars.umn.edu/

U.S. Census Bureau (2010a). *2010 census shows American's diversity: Hispanic and Asian populations grew fastest during the decade*. Retrieved from https://www.census.gov/newsroom/releases/archives/2010_census/cb11-cn125.html

U.S. Census Bureau (2010b). *Summary file 1. Asian alone or in combination with one or more other races, and with one or more Asian categories for selected groups, PCT7*. Retrieved from www.census.gov/2010census

U.S. Census Bureau (2012). *U.S. Census Bureau projections show a slower growing, older, more diverse nation a half century from now*. Retrieved from http://www.census.gov/newsroom/releases/archives/population/cb12-243.html

U. S. Department of Education. (n.d.). *Federal TRIO programs 2011 annual low income levels*. Retrieved August 27, 2014, from http://www2.ed.gov/about/offices/list/ope/TRIO/2011-low-income.html

Vander Putten, J. (2001). Bringing social class to the diversity challenge. *About Campus, 6*(5), 14-19.

Walpole, M. (2007). *Economically and educationally challenged students in higher education: Access to outcomes* (ASHE Higher Education Report No. 33:3). San Francisco, CA. Jossey Bass.

Ward, L., Siegel, M. J., & Davenport, Z. (2012*). First generation college students: Understanding and improving the existence from recruitment to commencement*. San Francisco, CA: Jossey-Bass.

Weber, L. (1998). A conceptual framework for understanding race, class, gender, and sexuality. *Psychology of Women Quarterly, 22,* 3-22.

Xie, Y., & Goyette, K. (2003). Social mobility and the educational choices of Asian Americans. *Social Science Research, 32,* 467-498. doi: 10.1016/S0049-089X(03)00018-8

Xiong, Z. B., Detzner, D. F., & Rettig, K. D. (2001). Southeast Asian immigrant parenting practices and perceptions of parent-adolescent conflicts. *Journal of Teaching in Marriage & Family, 1,* 27-48. doi: 10.1300/J226v01n01

Xiong, Z. B., Eliason, P. A., Detzner, D. F., & Cleveland, M. J. (2005). Southeast Asian immigrants' perceptions of good adolescents and good parents. *The Journal of Psychology, 139,* 159-175.

Xiong, Z. B., & Huang, J. (2011). Predicting Hmong male and female youth's delinquent behavior: An exploratory study. *Hmong Studies Journal, 12,* 1-34.

Yates, P. [Producer & Director]. (1979). *Breaking away* [Motion picture]. United States: 20th Century Fox.

Yeh, C., & Inman, A. (2007). Qualitative data analysis and interpretation in counseling psychology: Strategies for best practices. *The Counseling Psychologist, 35,* 369-403.

Yosso, T. J. (2005). Whose culture has capital? A critical race theory discussion of community cultural wealth. *Race, Ethnicity, and Education, 8,* 69-91.

About the Authors

Rashné Jehangir is an associate professor in the College of Education and Human Development at the University of Minnesota-Twin Cities. She began her career working with first-generation students in the TRIO Student Support Services Program. Her research interests focus on experience of low-income, FG students; multicultural curriculum and identity development; learning communities; and the design and structure of first-year experience programs. Current research projects employ visual mediums, specifically photos and film, to explore how narrative pedagogy impacts students' learning and development outcomes in college. Jehangir teaches in the First-Year Experience program in the College and advises graduate students in higher education and postsecondary teaching and learning. Her scholarship is featured in several journals, including *Journal of College Student Development, Innovative Higher Education, Urban Education,* and the *Journal of the First-Year Experience and Students in Transition,* as well as her book, *Higher Education and First-Generation College Students: Cultivating Community, Voice and Place for the New Majority* (2010). She has been invited to speak at several faculty and staff development institutes around the country and has presented at numerous conferences, including ASHE, FYE, AACU, and NCORE. Jehangir is on the editorial board for the *Journal of the First-Year Experience and Students in Transition* and *Learning Communities Research and Practice.*

Michael J. Stebleton is an associate professor in the College of Education and Human Development at the University of Minnesota-Twin Cities. His teaching and research interests focus on multicultural student development, college student success, and retention issues of historically marginalized student populations. Current studies focus on understanding the experiences of first-generation and immigrant college students. Stebleton teaches in the First Year Experience program in the College and also at the graduate level. His publications appear in a variety of academic journals, including *Journal of College Student Development, Journal of College and Character, Journal of College Student Retention, Journal of Student Affairs Research and Practice, Journal of College Counseling, Community College Review, NACADA Journal,* and others. He is also lead author on a career textbook, *Hired,* published by Pearson. Stebleton is an active member of ACPA and NASPA professional associations.

Veronica Deenanath is a doctoral student in the department of Family Social Science at the University of Minnesota-Twin Cities. She holds an MA in family social science, and her thesis was titled "First-Generation Immigrant College Students: An Exploration of Family Support and Career Aspirations." Deenanath's research interest focuses on first-generation college student success, immigrant families, financial capability, and money management.